Raise Your Hand

Hand

if...

Mike Sena, CFP®

Mike Sena, CFP® accepts a limited number of speaking engagements each year at conferences, associations, seminars and webinars. Please direct your requests to the author by email to mike@whitestreetadvisors.com.

ATTENTION CORPORATIONS, UNIVERSITIES, COLLEGES, AND PROFESSIONAL ORGANIZATIONS: Quantity discounts are available on bulk purchases of this book for educational, gift purposes, or as premiums for increasing magazine subscriptions or renewals. Special books or book excerpts can also be created to fit specific needs. For information, please contact White Street Publishing.

Copyright © 2013 by Mike Sena, CFP®
Front and back cover design © 2013, Katherine Gettys
Author photo by Paul Courtney

Published by White Street Publishing
PO Box 204
Roswell, GA 30077

Printed in the United States of America.

Second Printing 2015

ISBN: 978-1482344868
ISBN-10: 1482344866

Acknowledgements

There are hundreds of very fine people, and a few not so fine, that have helped me get to where I am today and complete this book.

A short list...

Tara Lane for being the first to plant a seed, she liked my writing. Stephen Monahan, Tanya Stewart, Esq. and Mark McGraw for their superb coaching, keeping me on track, in purpose and on my deadlines. Katherine Gettys for her enduring patience and always listening. My parents for teaching me how to learn from my mistakes.

Special thanks to Jack Harney and my dad John Sena, superlative editors who searched for and found most every error in my proof.

And most important, my son Jake who inspires me each and every day.

Disclaimer

I hate disclaimers, but I must...

This book is designed to provide information about personal finance, money management strategies and my musings about life and living.

It is sold with the understanding that within the context of this book, the author and publisher are not able to provide legal, tax, accounting, investment or other professional advice. The writings contained herein are not a solicitation of any investment advisory services or an offer to buy, sell or exchange any securities.

All information contained within this book is believed to be correct, but accuracy cannot be guaranteed, and most of this book is the opinion of the author.

The purpose of this book is to educate and entertain the reader. The author and publisher shall have no liability or responsibility to any person or entity with respect to any loss or damage caused from action taken as a result of reading this book.

Raise Your Hand

if...

Mike Sena, CFP®

"What we see depends mainly on what we look for."

John Lubbock

Mike Sena, CFP®

Introduction

Raise your hand *if...*

- You know playing the lottery is stupid. It may be fun, but it will not fund your life.
- You know starting to save for retirement in your 20s rather than your 30s is the difference between a 7-figure nest egg and a 6-figure one. And starting in your 50s is not the best plan you've come up with, but better than no plan at all.
- You know you should have at least 3 months of expenses saved someplace *safe,* pay off your credit cards *in full* each month, and operate from a written plan, that'd be a *budget.*
- You know not to trust those TV advertisements..."Get rich quick with *no* money down" or "We'll completely eliminate your IRS debt" or even "There's $MILLIONS$ of free money from the government just for the asking *if only you knew where to ask"*.
- You are married, single, 30, 60, divorced, widowed, father, mother, step-father, step-mother, grandparent or grand-child and find that money, off and on, is the biggest source of anxiety and stress in your life. (Just put this in to be sure I got at least one hand raised...)

How many of you raised your hand at least once? Twice? How about all five times?

Being smart doesn't necessarily keep you from

doing something stupid. Our mind and our money are too often at cross-purposes. We know all of the above, we know money is a practical everyday reality of life and living, that it's really just a tool. Unfortunately, most of us are too close to our money, it's too *personal*. We allow our feelings and fears and mania to creep in and drive the bus when we least need them to. Each of us has a very distinct perception about the purposes of money, and boy do we have emotions when we spend it. Very few of us are comfortable managing money and many fail to make the most of it within the other priorities of their lives, keeping money close and dear as a measure of self-worth or happiness.

Why? Typically two reasons...

First, we want people to like us, and a projected illusion of wealth is like magnet and steel, drawing others toward us that might not otherwise take a second look. We all want to fit in, to be accepted and admired, some of us liked more than respected. And right or wrong, in America these days the primary social currency is affluence. Even the appearance of it. It's highly seductive, and can be ultimately destructive.

Second, we are busy. We are just trying to keep all the plates in the air without any one being fumbled. We walk on this earth with jobs and spouses and in-laws, with parents and kids and step-kids. We have houses, cars, credit cards, mortgages and pets. Some of us have teenagers, some of us have infirm parents, some of us have a suspicious mole or mysterious pain we wish would simply disappear.

So, we tune out what is hard to focus on. Or what makes us uncomfortable.

Want to know the secret of happiness, of making money and generating wealth? Great happiness? Big money? Significant wealth?

Lean in. Closer. I'll whisper the secret in your ear. No, I still need you closer...

The best way to be happy, make money and generate wealth is not to master your checking account. *It's to master your mind.* With a plan. A written plan. One that's flexible, for you and your circumstances.

In the movie "*City Slickers*", weathered and leathery trail boss Curly, played by Jack Palance, passes along something, a bit of wisdom, to the bereft and just-turned-39 Mitch Robbins, played by Billy Crystal. He passes along something about the secret of life, something that will change Mitch's outlook forever. As he holds up a gloved forefinger, Curly states, "*Just one thing*". Robbins, wanting more, asks, "*What's the one thing?*"

"*That's what you gotta figure out.*"

That's what we all have to figure out. *Our one thing.* Once we have a clear understanding of what's important, the real priorities in our life, then we can begin to make the most of what we have now, live in the present and feel comfortable about our money and our future.

Following are forty-eight stories written by me at

some point between 2007 and 2012, somewhat journal style. These stories reflect my perceptions, experiences and lessons over the years as financial planner, entrepreneur, business owner, husband and father, occasional athlete, and full-time member of the human race.

There's no Table of Contents. The book is organized by month, January through December, four stories per month, that were either written in that month sometime over the past four turbulent years or are somehow related to that month. None is longer than a few pages, so it's pretty easy to just pick up the book and read.

Part of my intent here is to slip you back in time, to re-live the wild rollercoaster ride we've all been on since 2007. As you read, remember your feelings, your fear, your ambivalence. It's all material to the process of making money, avoiding financial mistakes and living comfortably. I'll let you in on another little secret. One that you'll also have to lean in close to hear. Closer...

It's always been this way. And always will be. Though there are typically longer periods of calm and upward momentum, there will always be some calamity occurring, something unexpected happening. Life does not play out in an ever escalating straight line.

So, as you read think about *you*. Your life, your situation, your priorities, your individual rollercoaster ride. You are unique, a one-of-a-kind. It's your life and your money. Make a plan for you, one that fits your objectives and lifestyle.

Some good lessons *I've* learned? A few...

I can only control how I *respond* to something or someone, nothing else. I can't change the past, but I can damn sure influence the present and change the future. And I find most of us don't resist doing, only getting started. So get started. It's simply a matter of choice. You have to want something different *more* than you want to stay where you are. Are the decisions you make today taking you closer to your objectives, your purpose? What are you willing to pay to get what you want?

Every day is a choice. What's yours today?

Mike Sena, CFP®

January

"Lots of people go mad in January. Not as many as in May, of course. Nor June. But January is your third most common month for madness."

Karen Joy Fowler

My 11 Must Own Stocks for 2011

Well, it's 2011. A new year. A new year to *make money* in the stock market. Even George Bailey is optimistic.

Last year, my portfolio of 10 must own stocks returned a whopping 48.95%, far outpacing any of the broad market averages. How did you do?

My best pick was Netflix, which jumped more than 250%, from just over $50 a share at the beginning of 2010 to $177 at the end. My next best was Cummins. It more than doubled from $54 to $110.

Having been an astute investor for over 20 years, I have developed a proprietary screen that crunches 17 data points to help me select stocks that will grow dramatically over the next year. Let me share with you my 11 must own stocks for 2011...

The above hyperbole is just that....complete and utter BS. My personal portfolio and my client's portfolio did well last year, but not that well. I did not own any of the above mentioned stocks for either myself or my clients, though I wish I did. Such is the luxury of hindsight.

The financial press is expert in exciting the motor neurons in human brains to act, and act repeatedly. Most everyone has an agenda, that may or may not be helpful to you, that may not be in *your* best interest. Don't you for a moment even consider using one of these "must own" prognostications to build a portfolio. Don't fall for the hype, don't believe the rhetoric, know that the vast majority of these "must own" stock picks fail to outperform any index. At best, these lists can be starting points for further research and investigation, but for most of us a well-diversified, low-cost portfolio of index oriented mutual funds or exchange traded funds with regular and consistent additions will likely prove to be the best course of action. Once you have your core portfolio established, individual stocks and some actively managed mutual funds may be included, within the confines of a disciplined and well thought out strategy with at least a ten year time horizon.

Is there a way to use these multitudes of "expert predictions" to your advantage? Can you sift through the garbage to get to the gem? Perhaps. Most of the predictions will fall within a fairly tight range, a consensus. There's an adage in the mutual fund business, "no one ever got fired for buying IBM". The same holds for new year's predictions...very few will venture far outside of conventional wisdom. There will be some, however, that will be bold, contrarian and convincing, on both sides of the general consensus. You can use these to frame your expectations to a degree. Most of the outlier returns, the ones you want, will be in the least expected places. Outside of the consensus.

The absolute main thing to remember when building an investment portfolio is to keep in the forefront *your* particular situation, *your* particular time horizon, and *your* particular objectives. Don't let anyone *sell* you an idea or investment. But do look where no one else is looking, and act *if* it makes sense for you and your situation.

Note: Written January 2011

What To Do With The Urn

I met with a friend this morning who, bluntly, sells cemetery plots and cremation services. We ended up having a wandering and questioning conversation, both of us trying to come up with a plan to prod people to think and plan, just a little.

He told me two stories...

One was about an older woman who had tragically lost both her husband and son at the same time. The two were cremated, but she made no specific plans about what to do with their remains. Still laden with grief after a couple of weeks, the urns were simply left in her car, safe but out of sight. While shopping for groceries one evening, her car was stolen. Though eventually recovered, her auto was thoroughly trashed and cleaned out of any item of value...including her beloved husband and son.

The second story was about a middle-aged man whose wife had passed away four or five years previously. Her body had been cremated with the remains placed in a urn that he kept at his house. Eventually, he became romantically involved with a new woman, and had to finally deal with a more suitable and permanent location for his deceased wife; he had no idea what to do with her.

Both stories illustrate the importance of having *the* conversation now, *while you can*. No better time than the present to visit the issues surrounding our eventual demise. Tragedies happen every day, and will with certainty happen to each of us at some point in time; in my mind the real tragedy is not having a plan in ṛ that love ones acknowledge, understand and accept. Sit down *today* and start a conversation about your wishes, and their wishes. Execute a will, a healthcare power of attorney, and a healthcare directive for life-sustaining medical treatment. Appoint a personal representative to administer your estate, and don't be bullied or feel that a spouse or adult child is always the best choice for this responsibility. Write a letter that identifies the location of important documents. And pay a good estate planning attorney a few hundred dollars to assist you.

The main point of end-of-life planning is to make your death as easy, painless and inexpensive as possible for those you leave behind; if you mess it up, they will likely give you hell when they eventually catch up with you.

You're Approved!

Well, Suze Orman has launched her very own pre-paid debit card, branded "The Approved Card". Approved for what, do you think?

Suze has done a very good job over the years selling books and air time for CNBC and PBS, and to give her credit, educating lots of folks with fair, generic advice. Key word here is generic. Her advice is not specific to you. And let's face it, she *is* essentially an entertainer and author.

To get started, I am not a fan of debit cards at all. Here some of the basics...

1. Absolutely first on the list is the *fact* that a mistake or fraud with your debit card results in *cash* from your account, *your cash*, coming out. Even though there are protections against fraud, unauthorized use and plain old mistakes, the cash is still gone, and you have to deal with it.

2. Debit cards are a huge source of revenue for banks. Now, I am not against any money making enterprise, but you need to understand that debit cards are not provided out of the goodness of your bank's heart.

3. Any card, debit or credit, tends to encourage spending. Flatly, there is nothing like the emotion you experience when a crisp, fresh, hard-earned $10 or $20 dollar bill leaves your fingertips. You *feel* it. It's very personal.

4. Pre-paid debit cards, like Suze's, are laden with fees. Suze's card is not terrible, costing you $3 to open, and $3 a month just to have. She does offer some type of credit protection and credit reporting, so for the thin-file or no-credit file users, her card could be helpful. Most other pre-paid debit cards will nickel and dime you out of your money.

5. Debit cards are an awful way to pay for travel, rent-a-cars, etc. because the acceptor often will place a hold on your cash for *potential* expense. For example, when you rent a car, you're not really sure of the ultimate expense until you turn the car in and tally up all the incidentals, and the car rental companies know this and will protect themselves.

Pre-paid debit cards *might* make some sense for some of the millions of folks out there without a bank account.

That's about it. If you think a pre-paid debit card will help you, look to Wal-Mart as an alternative.

A secured credit card, one with low fees and a clear, written policy on when a standard credit card will be issued, is a better deal. With a secured credit card, you open a savings account with cash that secures the card use. For example, $500 in a savings account will get a $500 credit line. As you use the card and pay according to the terms, over time, say 6 months to a year, you will be able to qualify for a standard card and have access to your $500.

If you are committed to a card, and everyone should have something, an even better deal is a cash-back or rewards credit card. A good source for the best deals, and I prefer cash-back over airline miles or rewards, is Bankrate.com. And the best news for any credit card is any fraud or mistake is only a *charge* against an account, not *cash missing* from an account.

I make few guarantees, but two I do make are: Spending cash will limit your spending. Every time. And, the magic formula for generating wealth is behavior. If your behavior is misbehaving, you're in trouble no matter what kind of card you use.

A New Drag on M&A

M&A, mergers and acquisitions, has been a part of the business landscape since, well, since business began. It has occasionally been portrayed in the movies, such as *Working Girl,* though there was also a different kind of merger included there, and of course *Wall Street,* the iconic Oliver Stone motion picture that epitomized the excesses of the '80s, where master of the universe Gordon Gecko dared to utter, "Greed, for lack of a better word, is good".

We have witnessed horrible mergers, such as the insult-to-injury marriage of AOL and Time Warner, or Sprint and Nextel's rocky and tenuous relationship. Then, there have been jilted suitors such as Google's abject rejection by Groupon or Yahoo's thankless rebuff of loving overtures from Microsoft. Some mergers and acquisitions work out very well, increasing efficiencies and enhancing shareholder value. Possibly the best example here would be Warren Buffett's Berkshire Hathaway, or serial acquirer Danaher. And then there is the monthly staple of the financial press narrating either the evils or goodness of reverse mergers, most notably where a Chinese company merges with a seemingly defunct American company, essentially a shell, that happens to still have a listing on some American stock exchange, for the express purpose of utilizing that exchange listing.

In keeping with the above mentioned movie theme, let's remember a timeless line from Steven Spielberg's 1975 blockbuster *Jaws*, where a mainland reporter has the grim responsibility of warning an unsuspecting public..." *in recent days, a cloud has appeared on the horizon of this beautiful resort community, a cloud in the shape of"* a lawyer...

Fundamentally, a merger is where two or more companies combine their businesses. And, an acquisition is where one company buys another. It is often the grease on the wheels of capitalism, an inherent freedom in a well-functioning economy. Considering today's "overstuffed with cash" corporate coffers, M&A is likely to bloom as the global economy improves. Unfortunately, I read with dismay a piece in the Wall Street Journal, *"First, the Merger; Then the Lawsuit"*, that chronicled the rise in "shareholder" lawsuits over proposed merger or acquisition activity. Such lawsuits have proliferated in recent years, the numbers far outpacing the stock price returns of the companies involved. In heady days of 2006, just 5 years ago, some 27 deal-related lawsuits were filed. In 2010 more than 216 were filed. It seems to have become a profitable exercise for ligation attorneys that specialize in this type of securities law, earning upwards of $400,000 per suit. Not bad for a few briefs and vigorous legwork by paralegals. In essence, much of the practice amounts to a shakedown. Like *Bruce*, the man-eating silent patroller Great White shark from *Jaws*, these trial attorneys are looking for a tasty, elsewhere-looking and distracted lunch. One that comes at the expense of you and I, ordinary shareholders; we are picking up the tab.

Clearly there are legitimate and necessary legal challenges to "fair value" formulations and injurious dealings, but some way, somehow, I'd like to find a way to slow down the flow of money merely from one pocket to another, and focus on practices that actually produce something of value or right a genuine wrong. Loser pays, perhaps??

February

"I miss everything about Chicago, except February."

Gary Cole

Be Careful Out There...

What do Joe Montana, Ronnie Lott and Harris Barton have in common? Other than, of course, playing hit-em' rough and tough, muddy and dirty football? All three together on the same pro team at the same time? One of the most dominate NFL teams in the 1980s to early 1990s? I mean the San Francisco 49ers. Winners of Super Bowls in '81,'84,'88, '89 and '94. One of my favorite teams. Anyone? Anyone? Bueller? Bueller?

How about as partners in a multi-billion dollar investment house named HJR Capital, LLC.? HJR, the initials of the trio's first names, *was* an investment firm that invested client's monies in other funds, like hedge funds, private equity funds and venture capital. They parlayed their celebrity status, their respective and significant star power, to introduce and be introduced, to recruit investors and find investments. They were motivated, goal oriented and, for a while, highly successful. They knew lots of people. And lots more people wanted to know them. After all, who wouldn't want to rub elbows and swap stories with the likes of Joe Montana?

If you think about it, from a distant and discerning eye, would you want former pro football payers managing your money? And a fund of funds? Essentially a double dip on management fees, once for HJR and once for the various investment funds.

To add insult to injury, the trio actually made commitments to various funds and outside money managers for monies they had yet to collect. So, they borrowed what they needed from a Silicon Valley bank to satisfy that end while fervently prospecting and selling new investors to fill the opposite end. Can you see how this ends?

What people should understand, and I think very few do, is the financial services industry is just that. An industry. A manufacturer. Not particularly different from General Motors, Johnson & Johnson, DuPont or Boeing. The financial services industry manufactures financial products to sell. But because the products sold are so near and dear, so very much subject to individual fear and greed and dreams, most of us lose the objectivity we exercise when buying a car or pill or chemical or airplane.

The financial services industry as a whole is hyper-competitive, short-term focused and marketing oriented. It is blessed with an abundance of very smart, very motivated, very charismatic sales professionals. My advice, *Be careful out there*. Don't be swayed by star power. Don't be seduced by charisma. Check your ego at the door, and remember, this is about *your money and your life*. Not your esteem. Not to impress your friends with who you know or what you think you know. Don't lose your money over a slick and charismatic sales pitch.

How to tell if you are being sold?

Rule #1: Understand what you are buying and *why*. I mean really understand.

Rule #2: Simpler is almost always better.

Rule #3: Before committing to anything from a commission based salesperson, check with a fee-only advisor.

Rule #4: Realize that star power rarely makes money for anyone other than the star.

Be well...

An Instructive Story...

Anyone else having fun in the delightful weather we've been having so far this winter? The yellow crocuses are up, but I've yet to see any tulips. So, this story, one of my favorites, is perhaps a bit early, but is still instructive. Anyone know where I am going here?

Tulip Mania. It was one of the most dramatic investment bubbles of all time, one of the most destructive, and one of the silliest. It is often regarded as the first reported investment bubble, where greed and avarice simply overtook any reason. BTW, I believe that human beings have perpetuated and participated in any number of speculative trading bubbles since the beginning of time, perhaps another story for another time.

The tulip made its way to Europe in the middle 1500s, via an ambassador from Turkey. First in Vienna, and then on to the Netherlands, where it really took hold and flourished. Because of its deep and dramatic color, the tulip was unlike most any other flower that could be found in Europe, and its popularity flourished along with the effervescent Dutch economy. Everyone loved them, and soon, covet began to set in. Competition became fierce and one-upmanship became the order of the day.

Unfortunately, tulips are not particularly easy. They generally only bloom in April and May, and seeds from one will not produce a bloom similar to the parent flower, sometimes you get what you wanted, but most times not. You need bulbs to essentially clone a parent bloom, and the bulbs are only available during the flower's dormant period, typically June through September. To add to the frustration of the tulip enthusiast, the most popular tulips were "exotics", where the bloom exhibited a breaking pattern in the dense color. This breaking pattern was the result of a virus that afflicted the bulb, weakening it and slowing propagation.

As an accelerant to the spreading demand for tulips, flower traders began the practice of signing a promise early in the year to buy tulips at the end of the growing season from the growers. These contracts were then traded among other flower dealers, and then opportunists got involved. Short selling, that is speculating that the price of tulip bulbs would actually go down, was introduced as well. Sound like anything you have heard before?

By 1634, in part due to increased demand from the French, speculation grew. By the fall of 1636, even contracts for common bulbs began to rise inexplicably, and Tulip Mania reached its peak in the winter of 1636-1637, where some bulbs were trading up to ten times a day and for prices that were up to 15 times what a skilled laborer might earn in a year. Like a child's soap bubble floating magically along with the breeze and then mysteriously popping, the market just evaporated by February 1637. No clear definable reason can be found, though the bubonic plague was ramping up during this same period, and it seems likely that death, and the fear of death, was more distracting than taking delivery of tulip bulbs.

What's my point here? Bubbles and crashes are part of the human condition. They always have been and always will be with us no matter what governments, pundits, policy makers or individuals think or attempt. The fever that grips man's imagination and fuels his greed is infectious and spreads among the heard. Be clear about what you are doing and why.

The Paradox of Choice

Many years ago, my father used to build houses for a living. I remember that he offered his home buyers a choice of 4 paint colors...only 4. As a kid, my world was full of color, and I didn't understand. When I asked him why only 4 colors, he told me that too many options make people indecisive and unsure, and he was actually doing a service for them. I really didn't understand what he meant at the time, but like so many things my father taught me, I eventually did.

The world is full of paradoxes. One of the more perplexing is the paradox of choice. As humans, and particularly Americans, we tend to take our freedoms for granted, generally a good thing and something to yearn and strive for. Conventional wisdom and modern thinking asserts that the more the choice, the more the freedom, the better the welfare and good for the individual.

The reality, though, is a little different. We are often confounded by our freedom of choice; it abounds us and at times paralyzes us into inaction, or worse the path of least resistance.

This is particularly a problem with our money. We are bombarded with choice....how much and on what to spend, invest for the future, protect ourselves and our loved ones. The choices are overwhelming with consumer and lifestyle products, savings and investment options, life and health insurance, taxes and on and on and on. So often, we respond to a default choice or the easiest choice or the choice with the least paperwork or the choice with the loudest voice...so often, the wrong choice.

How do we escape the paradox of choice?

Recognize it. Take actions for ourselves that tunes out the excess. Turn off the TV, shut off the video game, save the beer for later. Learn and educate ourselves to the point at which we know what choices are really in our best interest, what is in our power, control and expertise and what is not. We begin to understand that we don't know what we don't know. And for what is not in our expertise, we look for and find someone to help: a trusted advisor, insurance professional, tax professional, lawyer, etc. And we don't take their word or advice blindly...we take the time to understand our options, and be sure that our needs and desires are understood by those that serve *us*.

Because at the end of the day, we want to use our power

of choice wisely, to enhance our lives, not diminish them.

Debt Slaves

In Greek mythology, there lived a king who displeased Zeus to no end. This king had it all. He was the founder and first ruler of Corinth, a strategic and wealthy city-state that connected the major regions of Greece. He was father to four boys, and husband and lover to a most beautiful young woman. He promoted commerce and navigation throughout his kingdom with crafty cleverness. But, he was also avaricious and deceitful to his core. He murdered travelers and guests, committed incest with his teenage niece, and took pleasure in doing so. This king thought he was so clever, so utterly smart that he could rival and out-maneuver Zeus Himself.

So, who was this king?

Why Sisyphus, of course. And Zeus, more than a match for poor Sisyphus, extracted a cruel and devilish punishment for Sisyphus' betrayal of a secret in exchange for a new source of water. A punishment that seems to have lived on, and afflicts so many of us today. Zeus forced Sisyphus to roll a huge boulder up a steep hill only to have the boulder roll back down just as it almost reached the top. It was an endlessly frustrating and utterly useless task, like digging a hole in one place only to fill it in and do it all over again. And again.

Ever feel like Sisyphus? Like no matter what you do, you never seem to make any progress? I know a few folks who do, particularly when it comes to debt. They are debt slaves, imprisoned by their continued spending habits. Well, spending habits, like any other habit, can be changed. Not saying it will be easy, but in the immortal words of Yoda, "Try? Try not. Do. Or do not."

Want to get out of debt? Well, the first step is to be in *more pain with the debt* than the pain of change. Once you hit that point, it is much, much easier to proceed.

Second, you have to have an understanding of where you are financially. So, take all of those bills, statements, invoices, pay stubs, etc. out of the drawer and organize them. Turn off the TV, close down the Xbox, and make a list of your debts. Add up all of your fixed expenses, such as mortgage or rent, utilities, food, transportation, insurance and the like. Then compare that number to the bottom line on your pay stubs. Hopefully, the number on the pay stub is higher. If not, you have to do some soul searching...what are you going to give up?

Next, list your debts smallest to largest. Ignore for the most part the interest owed. Pay the minimums on all but the smallest, and attack that one with a vengeance, with purposeful intent. Once you have paid it off, you will get an emotional release. You have made an accomplishment. Move down the list to the next smallest and do the same...attack it until it is paid off. Repeat.

Most people that go through this exercise will never go into debt again. They remember the pain, the sleepless nights, the unease deep in their belly. Don't be like Sisyphus.

March

"It was one of those March days when the sun shines hot and the wind blows cold: when it is summer in the light, and winter in the shade."

Charles Dickens

Lizard Brains in a Silicon Age

Over drinks and dinner a couple weeks ago, a good friend of mine and I were able to make remarkable progress on solving our country's most pressing problems: health care, Iran, Afghanistan, the economy, Ted Kennedy's senate seat...

Once we settled with the bigger picture, we moved on to the more mundane and personal. I jokingly remarked that I had become convinced that human beings are not all that good at all when it comes to picking their mate and managing their money. My friend replied that he had always done an excellent job with his money, until he got married.

I'm not about to get into the former, but I do know something about latter, personal finance and managing money. And I'm here to tell you that the deck is stacked against most of us when it comes to our own financial well-being. Why is it that we make such poor decisions about money, and if we are really unable to make good decisions, why bother at all?

The first why, why do we make poor financial decisions? For most of us, money is a deep, mysterious, and emotional facet of our very selves. It often encompasses onion-like layers of distrust and discomfort and intense personal intimacy. Let's face it, you can't get any more personal without taking your clothes off. Combine this deep mysterious intimacy with the vast array of complex financial products and dozens of emotionally charged financial decisions involving life, death and taxes we have to make, and it is no wonder that most of us make less than satisfactory decisions.

Behavioral economists have been studying issues surrounding our hapless financial decision making for some time. There have been all sorts of studies and experiments exposing and explaining our built-in biases, genetic hard-wiring and the ever unsteady coping with the greed and fear pendulum. The last few years or so have been a veritable petri dish of revealing development and discovery, a living laboratory so to speak. To summarize their findings, our brains are essentially stuck in the stone age, at least the part controlling most financial decision making. Our lizard-like brains are trying to cope in an silicon age; we simply have not evolved our financial decision making apparatus to match the demands of 21st century life.

The main problem here, and naturally I'm only talking about those not reading this book, is that we're not rational. We think we are, but we're not. And the sooner we come to realize this, the better our decisions will be. For proof, just look back over the past three years or so. Was government, Wall Street and Main Street acting rationally? We are emotional beings with a fight or flight brain bombarded with a deluge of slick messages and conflicting information from the sublime to the ridiculous, all designed to evoke some sort of emotional response or action. Emotionally, we want to invest in that new hedge fund that is doing so well, we want to buy that hot stock or mutual fund, that new car, that new dress, that new boat or motorcycle, it feels good, Retailers, and let's be clear here, many financial "advisors" are retailers, are professional at getting us to part with our money. Add to this the Lake Woebegone effect, we all tend to think we are above average in smarts, looks and abilities, and as such we think we make above average and smarter decisions. Don't you?

Good planning and smart investing is about seeing the future, not reliving the past or expecting some cycle or trend to return. We need a realistic telescope with an objective lens. The best investment returns are almost always where you least expect to find them. So many times you have to lift up the carpet and blow the dust bunnies around to see more clearly what others are missing. Where do you think the good returns will be five years from now? Ten years from now? In other words, will you be surprised five or ten years from now looking back to today? Will you be kicking yourself and moaning "Any damn idiot could have seen it"? The best investors are able to remove today's fear and greed, and with steely nerves look forward. A splendid rule of thumb is to look where others are not, avoid the herd mentality, most mutual fund managers, CNBC and the relatively recent past performance. Recognize that financial well-being is a combination of behavior, attitude and purposeful action within an objective forward looking strategy that makes sense and fits your individual situation. Learn to enjoy what you have now, have a measure of contentment now, balance your reality with your emotional self.

Here's an interesting fact to think about: On the morning of September 11 2001, the Dow Jones Industrial Average was set to open at 9605. On the afternoon of September 11 2009, the DJIA closed at 9605. Pretty remarkable and pretty coincidental. There's been a lot of talk about the "lost decade". How does it make you feel? Does it make you feel mad or cheated or confused? Does it make you feel "why bother, what's the point?"

The point is that as human beings we must achieve, we must aspire, we must have goals. Without a goal, a direction, we will hit nothing, we will go nowhere. Without a useful purpose, we feel useless. The very essence of humanness requires us to seek more than we have. So given our inherent limitations, how do we achieve smart financial decision making? There are two answers: either develop a very rational way of thinking that will diminish our capacity for feeling and emotion, like a Warren Buffet, or seek an objective, competent and trusted advisor to help us along the way with the development of a strategy that minimizes financial mistakes and makes sense for our objectives and time horizons and situations.

A final thought: any person only invested in the DJIA is an idiot without any strategy.

Price Is What You Pay...

I had coffee with friends the other morning. We sat outside of a Starbucks, soaked in the warm spring morning and enjoyed pleasant conversation. Talk eventually got around to my business and the stock market. They were interested in my opinion of a few mutual funds and a couple of stocks. The stocks they were most interested in were Colgate Palmolive and United Parcel Service. Both are very fine companies, but do either make sense to buy now? How about we take a look...

- Colgate...the stock price has moved between $79 and $96 a share over the past 7 months or so, and today is trading at just under $96. The company pays a dividend of $2.48 per share annually, which equates to dividend yield of around 2.6% (dividend divided by share price).
- UPS...the stock price has moved between $61 and $82 a share over the past 6 months, and is trading today at $76 and some change. The company pays a cash dividend of $2.28 per share, which is around a 3% yield.

If you think about it, does it make sense that the business these two companies do would have changed so much in such a short amount of time? Less than 1 year? Yet the market, that is human beings, valued the total worth of Colgate between $37.8B and $46B...almost a *$10,000,000,000* difference, and UPS between $59B and $77B...an incredible *$18,000,000,000* difference. That's billion, with a B. All within a 6 or 7 month period. What was really different inside these companies last fall? Were business prospects really that dire? Really nothing, and really no. The point that I am making here is that when you buy, the price you pay makes a huge difference in your ultimate profit. Today, the market is doing well, and people are buying. Last fall, the market was doing poorly and people were selling. Why?

There have been countless studies that show *investments* typically do much better over time than *investors.* For reasons that are both deep and psychological *and* mired in our everyday realities of fear, love, rejection, worry and life, people are generally irrational when it comes to making money.

When you want to invest in the stock market, think about how you shop for food or gasoline or even socks. You look for things on sale, things selling at a bargain price. In the stock market however, too many decisions are made out of emotion, how we feel at that moment. And when we feel good about the stock market, when prices are rising, we buy. When we feel scared at falling prices, we sell. Just the opposite of what we should do.

If you want to make money in the stock market, you have to be cold and dispassionate. Every buy or sell has to be a business decision.

I think Colgate and UPS are very fine companies, but I have no interest in buying either one of them today or tomorrow. Who knows about 6 months from now...I stole a saying, "price is what you pay, value is what you get" (Warren Buffett).

What Are the Differences Between the Wealthy and the Poor?

So what are the main differences between the wealthy and the poor? *And a distinction I make is that wealth does not necessarily mean just money....*

Actually, a host of things separate the wealthy and the poor, but almost all relate to attitude and perspective. In my experience, most wealthy individuals approach life with a healthy and positive outlook, and most achieve their own success by helping others achieve success first.

The wealthy tend to have a much longer time horizon; they don't focus on today or tomorrow, but on next year, five years, twenty years from now. And with that long term focus, the wealthy avoid debt and spend money more wisely on things they need rather than want, they can put off certain wants until they can actually afford them, or in some cases find out that they really didn't want them after all.

Another difference is that the wealthy tend to think about how to make money rather than how to spend money. They are more turned on by solving problems, being flexible and innovating. I was talking with an associate last week who happened to mention that rather than outraged over the unprecedented level of spending out of Washington, he was reading parts of the newly signed stimulus bill to figure out how to get investment money. It turns out The Department of Agriculture has tens of billions of more money to spend, let your imagination roam...

I could go on and on, there are hundreds of books and videos on this topic, but the short and easy answer is, if you want more wealth in your life, start thinking more like the wealthy. And it really can be that easy. The fact is that the main difference between you today and five years from now will be the books you read, the people you meet, the classes you take and the *way* you think. Surround yourself with competent and positive people, develop a plan and get to it. There are plenty of resources and people able and willing to help you that are right at your fingertips if you just extend your hand.

A Tale of Three Woes

Investing can be perilous, particularly for the fearful, greedy or uninformed.

Three tales of woe to point out the importance of doing your homework, understanding all you can and keeping your brain and emotions in check...

#1...Remember the .com boom? Stock prices went through the roof just by adding .com or some "tech" imagery to a company's name. Made no difference how the business was doing or even if it made any money. Today, companies are doing the same thing, only with adding "China" to their name. Jason Zweig in the Wall Street Journal wrote a piece about just this. He and a finance professor at Queen's School of Business in Ontario, Canada, Wei Wang, looked at the returns of 82 companies that adopted new names containing "China" since 2006. Wang studied returns from 20 days prior to the announcement through 20 days after and found the "changed" company's stock price outperformed the overall market by some 31%. Zweig reports other examples of "name changes" to artificially pump up a stock price.

#2...How do you know if an active mutual fund manager who is beating the market is really skilled or just lucky? The fact is, you really don't. In fact, statistically you need around 55 years of performance data to be sure. One quick place to look, however, that can provide a few clues is the benchmark the manager uses to gauge his/her performance. Occasionally, fund managers will cheat a little on performance by comparing the fund's returns with a not so appropriate benchmark, say a

mid-cap value oriented fund may benchmark against the S&P 500...not too fair. Be sure you are comparing apples to apples as best you can when considering active management mutual funds. Read the prospectus to know what you are buying and figure out the best-fit benchmark. For funds that have generally outperformed their appropriate benchmark for at least 10 years, think about what might happen if he/ she leaves the fund. Better yet, put most or all of your money in low-cost index oriented funds.

#3...There has been a huge flight-to-safety over the past couple of years. Some investors have become so risk-averse that they blind themselves to the realities of their own situation and genuine objectives. A group of products has proliferated to meet this "need for zero-risk", generically called guaranteed principal investments. These financial products are engineered to guarantee your initial investment, or principal, and also provide some sort of upside potential if the market, say the S&P 500, does well. Sounds enticing, doesn't it? Well, there is no free lunch. These products require that you lock-up your money for a specific period of time, generally one year at a minimum and I have seen some that want a five-and-one-half year commitment. They are complicated, with pages of conditions and hard to understand wording. For the most part, they are made up of risk-free investments, such as Treasury Bonds, and long-term options, derivatives, on a particular benchmark, such as the S&P 500. They limit your upside, say 60% to 65% of the gain and they don't pay any of the dividends. And they can pose serious income tax inefficiency depending upon just how they are structured due to imputed income at ordinary income tax rates. The financial companies pushing these

products are going to make money with them, understand that. They are playing upon your fear. You can do pretty much the same thing on your own without locking up your money and without the extra expense.

Be careful out there; it's a jungle with all types of products and services being *sold*. Best to remember that simpler is better, complete understanding helps prevent costly disappointments and being *sold* on something typically only helps the seller.

April

"The first of April is the day we remember what we are the other 364 days of the year."

Mark Twain

Tax Day...

Tax day cometh, too juicy an opportunity to let slide by without comment. So let's dive right in, shall we...

The income tax was first used in this country in 1861 to help finance the War Between the States. It was a flat tax of 3% on annual incomes over $800. It lasted only a year and expired. Congress, recognizing a good thing when it saw it, couldn't leave well enough alone and replaced it with a graduated tax of 3% to 5% on annual incomes over $600. The Congress has had an on-again, off-again love affair with it ever since.

Our current tax code, so named Title 26 of the United States Code, was set up by the Sixteenth Amendment to the Constitution, which was passed by Congress in 1909 and eventually ratified by the states in 1913. The main purpose of the Sixteenth Amendment was to settle a squabble between the Courts and Congress over forms of income that could be taxed. Article 1 of the Constitution specifically limited Congress' ability to impose *direct* taxes, which are taxes on property or persons, by requiring Congress to distribute such direct taxes in proportion to each state's census population. So, the new amendment formally allowed Congress "to lay and collect taxes on incomes from whatever source derived..."direct, from property, or indirect, from wages". Initially, income was taxed between 1% and 7% depending upon just how much one earned. Tax rates have changed 39 times since and have ranged from 0% to 94% of taxable income. We now endure 6 individual tax brackets, 5 individual filing statuses, a "kiddie" tax, a completely separate and parallel tax called the Alternative Minimum Tax, 5 tax brackets on estates and trusts, a moving target on death taxes, 2 different capital gains tax rates plus another rate on collectibles.

The income tax has morphed into a modern day Frankenstein. And like Frankenstein, it is a monster of epic proportions, stitched together like the hands and fingers and feet and head and abnormal brain that made dear ole' Frankie so loveably grotesque. There are some 15 sections within Title 26, written with close to 10 million words, 10 MILLION, that is like a book thirty inches thick, too ponderous and dense to carry in your hands.

At this point, another favorite monster of old comes to mind, the nefarious and diabolical Count Dracula. Just like the blood-sucking Count, our tax system sucks, sucking productivity out of you and me. In 2010, we will spend an estimated $368B on compliance, some 23% of federal expenditures. That's about $1200 for every man, woman and child living in America. Another way of comparison is to go back in time and look at the tax code in 1990. Then, there were only about 5M words to instruct us on how, when and where to pay taxes, and compliance costs were estimated to be around $80B. It seems that the tax code has even outperformed the stock market over the past twenty years.

Well, complaining never got anyone anywhere. The best anyone can do is to understand the code, otherwise known as The Accountants and Politicians Retirement Security Act (not really, just a joke, particularly for those of us without a sense of humor, Lord knows we all need a sense of humor here), as well as possible and use it the best we can...

The majority of taxes collected by the U. S. Federal Government are from levies upon income earned by individuals. All income will eventually be classified as either "ordinary" or "capital".

Ordinary income refers primarily to income we earn through work from an employer or self-employment. This type of income is also referred to as "earned" income. Certain types of savings and investment income, often referred to as "unearned" or sometimes "passive" income, are also classified as ordinary. This income includes interest we earn from savings accounts, certificates of deposit, interest from loans to others (including companies or governments, as in a bond), income realized from the sale of capital assets held for less than one year, and certain other investments. Ordinary income will be taxed at a progressive tax rate that increases as your income increases. As of today, ordinary income tax rates begin at 10%. They then increase progressively with income to 15%, then 25%, then 28%, then 33% and end at 35%.

The progressive nature of our income tax code is the reason you hear or see the term "marginal tax rate". Marginal refers to only the top portion of our income taxed at the highest rate. For example, if you are married and file your taxes returns jointly with your spouse and your total taxable income is $100,000, your income tax will be 10% of the first $16,050 ($1605) *plus* 15% of the next $49,050 ($7357.50) *plus* 25% of the next $66,350 up to your total income of $100,000 ($8725), or a total of $17,687.50. Even though your *average* income tax rate is 17.6875%, your marginal tax rate is 25% because you pay a portion of income tax at that rate and each additional dollar you earn will be taxed at that rate.

Capital income refers to gain or profit from capital assets. Capital assets include investments such as stocks, mutual funds, Exchange Traded Funds (ETFs), investment real estate, a personal home or vacation home, and the like. If you hold a capital asset for longer than one year, a typically more preferential tax rate will be levied on the profit or gain. This preferential tax rate is called a long term capital gains tax rate. Long term capital gains tax rates as of today will generally be either 5% or 15%, depending upon the taxpayer's marginal income tax bracket. For marginal income tax brackets of 15% or less, the long term capital gains tax rate is 5%. For marginal income tax brackets of 25% or more, the long term capital gains tax rate is 15%.

Any income from a capital asset held less than one year will be taxed as ordinary income at ordinary income tax rates rather than long term capital gains tax rates.

Due to a fairly recent change in the tax code, most dividends received from common stock ownership are also taxed at the preferential long term capital gains tax rate. Dividends are cash payments made to stockholders from profits earned by a company.

Any distribution from a tax deferred annuity or tax favored retirement account will be taxed at ordinary income tax rates, regardless of what kind of asset is inside the annuity or account.

Typically, the standard deduction, personal exemptions and the amount of income within each tax bracket will rise with the cost of living each year.

The current tax code is amazingly complex, changes

frequently and is subject to differing interpretations by differing bodies. I use terms like "most", "typically" and "generally" when discussing or outlining aspects of tax regulation because there is almost always an exception or "gotcha" to any IRS rule. It is always easier to formulate and implement a tax efficient strategy as part of an overall plan *before you take any actions.*

Note: Written April 2010; tax rates have changed...

Losing Your Shorts

On the morning of December 11, 2008, a well-dressed, confident and handsome guy boarded a flight from New York to Los Angeles. Upon entering the plane, he took an abrupt left, strolling into first class. Having built a solid and profitable business over the years, and enjoying a flush checking account, he had become accustomed to the cozy comforts in the front of the plane. While fiddling the time away, his eye was tugged toward the bottom of his adjacent video monitor. The monitor was tuned to CNBC, and a breaking news story was crawling across the bottom of the screen. The crawl stated that in what appeared to be the world's largest financial fraud and Ponzi scheme, authorities had arrested Bernard Madoff. He just stared dumbly, trying to take this in. He remembers thinking, "No, no...that can't be right." But, the crawl appeared again, and the reporters and reporterettes were breaking away to live coverage of this unprecedented happening. He calmly gathered himself. He folded his soft, white linen napkin and placed it on the seat armrest. He unbuckled his seatbelt, stood up and then made his way to the back of the plane. He addressed the flight attendants milling in the rear galley, "I'll be getting off now. Would you mind opening the door? I don't need a parachute."

Adding a bit of literary license, this is how Harry Markopolos begins the financial thriller *"No One Would Listen"*, his account of pointing the finger of fraud and deceit at Madoff since 1999.

So, how did this guy, the one that wanted to get off the airplane before its scheduled arrival, get taken? *He lost his shorts.* How did so many get taken by Madoff? There were 1000s of people who lost money, close to 350 different funds from across the globe were invested with Madoff, over $65B. That's *$65 BILLION*. And most important, how do *you* keep from being taken? How do *you* keep from losing your shorts?

I'll get to that in a minute.

First, I want to talk about Madoff.

Bernie Madoff is an amazing story. Born in Queens, NY, in 1938, descended from Jewish immigrants from Poland and Romania, the son of a plumber turned stockbroker, he was raised with a strong work ethic and an intense desire to succeed. Starting with nothing but the earnings from lifeguarding and installing sprinklers, and a loan and a few introductions from his accountant father-in-law, Madoff opened Bernard L. Madoff Securities, LLC in 1960 at the tender age of 22. Madoff was a market maker, a connector of buyers and sellers. He dealt primarily with Pink-Sheet issues, that is over-the-counter securities. He was driven, methodical and always thinking. Combined with this drive, he was affable, charismatic and instinctively knew how to cultivate relationships. In essence, he was an efficient machine that others trusted and liked. As his business grew, Madoff invested heavily in technology, pouring money back in to his company, developing one of the first electronic trading systems. This technology eventually formed the backbone of the NASDAQ stock exchange. There, Madoff was directly involved in its development and growth, and he also found his way to the Chairman of the Board of Directors of the NASD, the National Association of Securities Dealers, which was the self-regulating organization of broker-dealers (ironic, isn't it, that he stole from some of the very people that he was supposed to keep honest). His business became the largest market-maker on the NASDAQ, and the 6th largest overall on Wall Street. He was a prolific philanthropist and was politically well-connected, yet maintained a knack for discreetness. He was plenty wealthy, respected and admired, with no apparent reason to sociopathicly deceive others in such a dastardly ponzi scheme. So, why do it? And of all the folks that got taken, no one, not one, thought that they would lose money, primarily because of the same reasoning.

Which leads back to how you can avoid losing your shorts.

My first rule, the most important rule, the rule you must learn and never forget is...

1. Understand that you can be taken...

Repeat after me, "*I can be taken*". Say it again, "*I can be taken*". We all have a built-in and hard-wired cognitive bias that for most of us makes us more confident and superior than we really are. Think of Lake Wobegon, where everyone is above average. History is littered with the half-open and completely empty wallets belonging to very smart people that never thought it could happen to them. I get the feeling that many of you are still unbelievers. As a reinforcement, a dare so to speak, visit the website of a securities attorney that represents victims of financial fraud. Pat Huddleston was one of the few competent attorneys at the SEC, The Securities and Exchange Commission. He left there to start his own private practice, Investor's Watchdog, LLC. Pat writes a daily blog that chronicles all the ways that honest people lose their shorts, get taken. I dare you, read Pat's blog for two weeks. It will make a believer of you.

You are most susceptible when you least suspect it.

2. Never give your money to an advisor...

Never, ever, ever. Always use a third party custodian, someone like Fidelity, TD Ameritrade or Schwab to hold your money. If you want an advisor to manage your money, that's fine. Give him or her a discretionary trading power of attorney that allows them to make trades on your behalf, but does not give them access to your cash. You may lose all your money due to incompetence, but it will not walk out snuggly ensconced inside your advisors' pockets on a celebratory trip to the Mediterranean. By the way, there are more and more good fee-only advisors that *do not* offer a discretionary management option, just advice that *you* implement; something to consider.

Keep your cash close.

3. Understand what you are investing in...

One reason Madoff got away with what he did is that many people didn't understand what he was doing. He employed a complicated strategy, and only people that truly understood options, like Markopolos, could see that he was scamming people (an option is a financial contract that gives one the right to buy or sell a particular security at a particular price by a particular date). And Madoff's scheme used a complex combination of buy and sell options at various prices by various dates. Even the SEC couldn't understand his strategy, they investigated him in 2004/ 2005, and essentially gave him a clean bill of health because they hadn't an iota what he was up to. So many people don't really understand what they are buying. In the end, it is your responsibility to know what you have, to ask questions, to insist on meaningful and understandable answers. And then, to make sure what you have been told is truthful...remember that sage Cold War and teenage years maxim, "*trust but verify*".

If you don't understand it, don't do it.

4. If it sounds like a duck...

Yes, if it sounds like a duck, walks like duck, craps like a duck, then it probably is a duck. There are no free lunches on Wall Street, or anywhere else, outside of the US Capital cafeteria. Don't get greedy. When it comes to financial products and service, be wary of skillful players with pearly white smiles that make it sound foolproof and risk proof. Though there are plenty of reputable and trustworthy insurance agents, stock brokers and financial advisers, much of Wall Street is by design a huckster contest. I love the Warren Buffet line, "If after 5 minutes during a card game you can't figure who the patsy is, it's you". Don't get suckered in to a too-good-to-be-true deal.

Don't get greedy.

Certainly, there is no fool-proof system to remain safe. Life is not without risk. If, however, you exercise some common sense, recognize we all have built-in and hard-wired mental biases, don't give your money directly to anyone to invest for you, understand what you are investing in and why, and do not get greedy, maybe you'll get to keep your shorts.

Simpler is Better...

William lived adjacent to a small woodland village in Surrey, England during the late 13th to early 14th century. He was a Franciscan Friar. Friars are an order of the Catholic Church, and a Franciscan, founded in the early 1200s by Saint Francis of Assisi, was one of what is called the four "great orders". As a friar, William lived in service to his community rather than cloistered away like a monk. He was a theologian and logician, a thinker and a theorist. Mostly, William thought about people, the Church and his life around him. He is perhaps best known, at least to me, for a principle that bears his last name, Ockham (sometimes spelled Occam). Ockham's Razor is an idea that I have learned to incorporate into my life..."*Pluralitas non est ponenda sine neccesitate*", or "*Entities need not be multiplied beyond necessity*". In plainer English, when you have two courses of action or competing theories that achieve the same prediction, objective or outcome, you should prioritize your research and energies *first* on the simpler of the two. I have reduced his Razor a bit more...simpler is better.

How many of us needlessly complicate our own lives? Does the complexity and accompanying clutter, the physical, financial and emotional flotsam we accumulate and carry, enhance our time on earth or improve daily living?

At this point, I could go on and on citing needless and counter-productive complexity that occurs every day. Most of the mess we are in right now stems directly from the fact that too many people had too little understanding of just what in the heck they were doing, they relied on others to pass judgment on products that they could not or would not understand. But, rather than waste time and effort pointing out what is already known, I think it's better to persuade and convince you to remember Ockham and his Razor. Certainly government and Main Street should, Wall Street is not really designed to, another topic for another day, but two out of three would definitely help.

Practice will be necessary. We are born and trained to think and innovate, and too many of us equate thought and innovation with depth and complexity instead of better and simpler. Practice choosing the simpler alternative first, practice Ockham's Razor, and witness your life improve.

Particularly when it comes to money management, our built-in competitiveness and innovativeness spurs us on to progressively complex strategies designed to eke out just that little bit more, that slight edge over the competition. We want to prove to someone else or even ourselves just how damn smart we are. But so often, our innovativeness gets us in trouble, there is always the misunderstanding, the unintended consequence, the unexpected event, the blindside, someone with a different agenda roiling your design and spoiling your fun. And speaking of other people and human consequence, let's not forget a somewhat related principle, Hanlon's Razor..."*Never attribute to malice that which can be adequately explained by stupidity.*"...it's incredible how many smart people do stupid things. It's as if they simply open up their heads and remove their brains for specific periods of time every other day or so. Don't ever discount the impact of someone else's stupid-at-the-moment decision as it possibly impedes your strategy or your design.

When designing a strategy for your life, keep it simple. When designing an investment portfolio, keep it simple, too, and within your range of complete understanding. Don't let someone talk you into a product or service or security that doesn't make sense for your situation and circumstance or sounds too good to be true. For the most part, if we can avoid doing dumb stuff, we will be fine, staying out of trouble is a lot easier than getting out of trouble. I can't prove this with a formula or model, only provide anecdotes to the reality. Instinctively we know this is true, but our hard-wired, innovative-oriented thinking tends to override the keep-it-simple circuits. Simple strategies go a long way to help us stay out of trouble.

Towards that end, I have come up with a short and easy to remember list of five undeniable truths to help keep me on track:

Life is not fair.

People are not rational.

There's always the unexpected.

Be grateful for what is.

And, Simpler is better.

The Art of Practice

I remember when I was a youngster and becoming interested in girls, how nervous I would get at the mere prospect of picking up the telephone to call one. My stomach would get queasy, my skin would get clammy, I would become interested all of a sudden in doing my chores, anything but picking up that telephone and dialing her number...

Luckily, I had a friend that lived across the street, not quite a best friend, but a good friend. He was somewhat of a mentor to me. He was Mr. Smooth in my eyes, polished, glib, athletic, good looking and very successful with the ladies. At some point, I confided my fears to him, and he looked at me and said rather directly that whenever he wanted to call a girl, particularly one he didn't know very well, he would think of what he wanted talk about, plus a few other conversational items, and write them all down. He would then practice saying them over and over until he was comfortable. Then he would place his call and work his charms.

I was absolutely dumbfounded at the notion that someone as smooth as my friend actually practiced his craft. I tried it, and amazingly, it worked for me too, just a little practice before-hand and I became much more comfortable calling anyone anytime about anything.

Fast forward several years to college. I lived with a guy who in time had become my best friend. He was a terrific guy who I enjoyed living with and cavorting about. His truly great gift was storytelling. I mean he could spin a yarn or tell a joke and have everyone in rapt attention, anxiously awaiting the next twist in the plot or delivery of the punch line. I marveled at how talented he was.

One afternoon, I came home unexpectedly from class and heard him talking in his room. I wandered in to see who was there with him, and found him facing the mirror telling a joke, a joke I had heard him tell the previous evening. When I asked him what in the heck he was doing, he replied that he was having trouble getting the punch line just right. So, he was practicing in front of the mirror.

Once more, someone I knew pretty well who was really good at something I aspired to actually had to work at it and practice it. I think I am starting to learn something here. I starting practicing my jokes and stories, and I got better and more comfortable.

The fact of the matter is you don't get anywhere without practice. Malcolm Gladwell, in his new book "*Outlier*",, differentiates between average, skilled and accomplished expert, essentially by the quality and amount of practice. After looking closely at the lives of Mozart, Bill Gates, Bill Joy, The Beatles and others, he asserts that it took each of them around 10,000 hours of practice to become truly expert in their field. Think about that number, 10,000 hours.

Now, I find that most of us tend to hate "practice". We hate the word and we hate the process. I know my son does. Practice conjures up visions of repetition, boredom, no fun. Particularly when that practice takes us a little out of our comfort zone. Take us much further out of our comfort zone, then real panic can set in. And the uncomfortable truth is that failure is inevitable, it is part of essence of being human. But, add in a little zest, a little imagination, a little vision, picture yourself as you want to become, and practice can become an art, something to embrace where you actually enjoy the process, challenge and exhilaration that comes from stepping beyond yourself from time to time to expand your abilities and horizons. So practice, and get better at whatever it is that you either enjoy or need to get better at. And don't mind the inescapable mistakes and little failures, live a little and take pleasure in being human.

May

"Rough winds do shake the darling buds of May,
And summer's lease hath all too short a date."

William Shakespeare

Foreign Flavor

Sunday night, *"Raiders of the Lost Ark"* was on TV. One of many memorable lines from the movie is Arnold Toht, sinisterly asking Miriam and Belloc, *"Now, what shall we talk about?"*

I gave a speech last week to the North Atlanta Rotaract Club, where I asked just that, "What do you want to talk about?" I got several in the audience to reply with good questions. One particularly good question was about Forex, or foreign currency trading.

Want to learn something about that? It is more interesting than I thought I knew...

Foreign currency is the largest trading market by dollar volume, with some $4T, that is *trillion,* changing hands every trading day. Trading begins at 10:00am Monday morning in Sydney, Australia and follows the sun west through trading centers across the globe. The market closes at 5:00 pm Friday in New York, allowing traders to speculate on currency values from anywhere in the world 24 hours a day, during the traditional work week, traders simply place their trades over-the-counter in whatever market happens to be open.

The vast majority of trades is by banks, with some 77% of all trades made by just 10 global banking institutions. Deutsch Bank is in the top spot with 15%+, and Morgan Stanley at the bottom with some 3.6%, according to a survey by Euromoney.

And, the United States dollar makes up some 85% of all trades, with the Euro coming in second with just over

39%, and the lowly Indian rupee at just under 1%. In case you are thinking and adding it up, the total percentage of currencies traded equals 200% because all trades are done in pairs, such as the American dollar to the Euro, or the Pound sterling to the Japanese yen.

Throughout any given day, information pours across news wires that cause minor fluctuations in the value of various foreign currencies relative to other currencies. Traders make, or lose, money by speculating on the rise or fall of this value. These values move relatively little compared with the fluctuating prices of common stocks or bonds, but the use of leverage, that is borrowing money to enhance returns, magnifies the returns, or losses, like an athlete on steroids pumping his legs to the finish line.

Trading currencies is not for the faint of heart, and certainly not for the uninitiated. There are several foreign currency brokers that will "teach" you how to trade currencies and let you practice with *fake,* or virtual, money. Trading with fake money is lot different than trading with *your* money. Trust me. And trading currencies is an education unto itself. If you know what you are doing, you can make a lot of money. If you don't know what you are doing, you will lose a lot of money. So, are you ready to trade?

Perspective or Perception?

I heard a story not too long ago, one that I had heard many years ago and had forgotten. It is instructive...

Back in the middle 1800s, when Great Britain was still a great empire, a shoe manufacturer in central London wanted to expand its reach, wanted to make and sell more shoes. Towards that aim, it dispatched two sales agents to Africa to scout out possible sales opportunities. Within a few days of arrival, the 1st agent wired back to the home office, "Situation hopeless...no one here wears shoes." The very next day, the home office received a wire from the 2nd sales agent, "Situation marvelous...no one here wears shoes."

Isn't it amazing how two different people can witness the exact same thing, and come away with vastly different perceptions? What a difference perspective makes...

Our perspective, that is our evaluation of a particular situation, is completely a matter of our perception, that is the use of our senses and past experiences to acquire and process information. Perhaps a subtle difference, but illustrative of the human condition. We are all different, with different life experiences that mold and shape how we view life unfolding around us.

When it comes to money, our perspective is intimately shaped by our perception of money, how we were raised, what money is and means to us individually. What is your perspective? Is it healthy? Does it help you get what you really want? Would you like to get more out of what you have?

Though my business and practice is to help individuals and families plan for the future, and *I do know that a plan is essential*, I find more and more that I am helping folks makes the most of what they have now and to live more in the present. Do you?

Something worthwhile to remember..."The past is history, the future is a mystery and today is a gift...that's why it is called the *present*" . Treat each and every day as a *present*, and your perspective and perception of money and what it does will change, will enhance your daily living. Try it and see...

Do You Need Alternative Investments?

In a word, maybe...

There has been a lot of talk lately about alternative investments. What is an alternative investment and do they help? Think ... hedge funds, managed futures, gold and other precious metals, absolute return notes, commodities, private equity, energy trusts, real estate partnerships and non-traded real estate investment trusts, art and other collectibles as alternative investments. The list is vast, and growing. The whole idea of alternative investments is to provide some diversification from stocks and bonds so that overall risk is reduced without reducing return.

I tend to avoid the hedge funds and managed futures. Hedge funds are expensive and it's hard to find a good one, and I think the jury is still out on managed futures. I have never been a strong advocate of gold or precious metals...gold has been hot lately but has barely returned much more than the rate of inflation since America went off the gold standard in the 1970s. The rest of the list, however, may make some sense for some people; as with any investment, a person's particular situation, objectives and time horizons dictate specific investments.

Absolute return notes are a manufactured financial product typically comprised of two components: a guaranteed return through a Treasury note or ultra safe bond and a futures contract based on the performance of a particular index such as the S&P 500 over say a 12 to 24 month time horizon. Absolute return notes typically guarantee your principal investment and offer upside potential based upon the performance of the particular index over a specified period of time. Like so many things, the devil is in the details so be sure you understand the risks and exactly how the note works.

Commodity investments are generally in the form of futures contracts; a bet on the future supply, demand and price of a commodity within a fixed time horizon. Commodities include things like oranges, bacon, coffee, timber, oil and natural gas, etc. Rather than bet on the future market of any specific commodity, I prefer to purchase stock in well-managed companies that are in the business of growing, harvesting, mining, drilling or refining, and distribution of commodities. Private equity companies buy private or public businesses, typically in distress, and typically finance the purchase with a lot of debt. There are also companies outside of commercial banks, business development companies, that specialize in providing financing to companies in need.

Energy trusts sell shares in income producing properties that are involved in the exploration, production and distribution of oil and natural gas. I think natural gas and pipelines may make some sense today.

Real estate partnerships are comprised of a knowledgeable and trustworthy general partner who invests cash from limited partners in various commercial income-producing real estate ventures. Typically, investments are committed for longer periods of time, up to say 10 years, and can provide monthly income, potential tax advantages and eventual return of principal. Non-traded real estate investment trusts sell shares that do not trade on an established market and generally pool large sums of money for larger and more diverse projects. Along the real estate theme, timber real estate investment trusts may also be a good fit for many investment portfolios.

Art, wine, automobiles and other collectables rarely make sense for most investment portfolios, unless there is some particular expertise. Also, count on a higher capital gains tax rate levied on the realized appreciation of collectables.

One last alternative that many people fail to consider, cash and cash equivalents. Cash and cash equivalents have a place in every portfolio, regardless of age, objective or time horizon. I remember well during the dot-com boom that many folks knew tech stocks were bound to fall at some time, but would not consider cash or U. S. Treasuries as an alternative. Well, we all learn.

Many investment portfolios can use a dose of

alternative investments, say between 5% to 20%. Team up with a fee-only advisor to help you decide if alternatives make sense for you. And never, ever invest your money without complete understanding of the investment and risks.

Don't Yawn...

I have a client that wants to expand our relationship. We started off with me only managing their money. But as their situation has changed, grown more complex, and with a new child on the way, we have been looking deeper and at other aspects of their lives that could play an important role going forward. One is disability insurance.

I can see your the back of your right hand involuntarily moving up to your mouth, hiding a yawn, while this book, in your left hand, is slowly sliding down to the desktop or your lap, and you're thinking of doing something else. Don't move away from this page just yet...

This particular client, the wife, was a contractor for a consulting company, performing various project management duties. Once she completed her MBA, the company hired her full-time. As such, she was became entitled to all the benefits the company offers to other full-time regular employees. So, she signed up for the company short-term and long-term disability insurance at the behest of the company's advisor on benefits, who happened to be an insurance agent. Not that there's always anything particularly wrong with that, and so far so good...

Where it gets interesting is she didn't know at the time she enrolled in the short-term disability plan that she was pregnant. And like most of us, never read the plan documents nor had any real understanding of what questions to ask. Once she became aware of the pregnancy, she wondered if she would be covered by the short-term disability, supposedly 60% of her base pay, and why she was not having any payroll deduction for her share of the premiums as of yet. Just curious, what do think the answer is to both those questions?

I ended up talking to the company's advisor, the insurance agent, but only about the company 401k plan (the disability insurance hadn't come up yet). He seemed competent and professional to me. I have no way of knowing how extensive his explanation of the total benefit package to my client was, as I wasn't there and have plenty of experience with clients, and most anyone, hearing only what they want to hear (one reason I always put in writing my understanding of any client or prospect conversation and ask for clarification if any). Here are some basics on employer provided disability insurance:

- It is typically generic, not specific to your needs and/or situation.
- If the employer pays the premiums, they are tax deductible to the employer and the benefits you receive are taxable to you.
- Most employer disability plans fall under the 1974 federal Employee Retirement Income Security Act, or Erisa—with a federal judge

ruling on disputes and no damages allowed for non-performance.
- Many employer disability plans have a rather strict definition of what a "disability" is.

So, how do think things will turn out for my client?

Well, one specific of her short-term disability coverage is a 90-day waiting period from her application for coverage before she is eligible. Another specific is a pre-existing condition is defined as one with recent medical care *prior to the date of eligibility* as opposed to the date of *application*. She is *not* going to get any maternity leave benefits from the short-term disability policy. The long-term portion, however, is a pretty good deal for her, and will go a long way towards making up for any lost wages due to an extended period of disability.

Four things I hope you will take away...

1. Short-term disability should be covered by you, that's what an emergency fund is for.
2. You are much more likely to become disabled for up to 5 years or more at some point in your life than to die prematurely. So, at the very least look at long-term disability insurance.
3. You absolutely have to read and understand the terms of any disability insurance, employer provided or not.
4. Always be wary of insurance agents advising you on insurance or investment products. Good or not, agents serve two masters, their bosses and then you.

June

"Spring being a tough act to follow, God created June."

Al Bernstein

Does Anyone Care?

With the recent publicity surrounding the charge of sexual assault, and the subsequent arrest, arraignment and bail of Dominique Strauss-Kahn, the managing director of the IMF, I wondered: Just what is the IMF, what is its function and should it matter to me?

The IMF, International Monetary Fund, was conceived in the waning days of World War II. In July, 1944, there was a convening of allied representatives at the Mount Washington Hotel located in Bretton Woods, New Hampshire. They wanted to talk about future regulation and financial order in a post-war world. The gathering was formerly called "The United Nations Monetary and Financial Conference", but is more commonly known and referred to as Bretton Woods.

The basic goal of the IMF was to make available emergency short-term loans with affordable terms to countries that got into economic trouble, and thereby hopefully discouraging the destabilizing and at times calamitous currency devaluations that had been the norm prior to WWII. Over time the IMF seemed to work fine, with devaluations rare and orderly.

The American dollar was fixed to the price of gold, dollars were convertible to gold and most currencies were tied to the dollar at a fixed rate. Then, in the early 1970s, Richard Nixon responded to rising inflation, a larger trade deficit and increased government spending due to social programs and the Vietnam War by canceling the direct convertibility of US dollars to gold, and taking us off of the gold standard. This effectively ended Bretton Woods and the original purpose of the IMF.

Of course, like all well-intentioned government programs that never seem to die, the IMF adapted to a new mission: To be a global economic fixer-upper. It has flexed its muscle, particularly as of late, and enjoys a wide mandate from its now 187 member nations. Its deliberations and decisions have become increasingly political and intended to be heard and understood by an initiated few, rather than practical, useful and transparent. It generally recommends currency devaluations (ironic, isn't it?) coupled with higher taxes as conditions to receive IMF backed loans. Critics maintain that such measures are counter-productive, and lead to less economic prosperity rather than more.

Does the IMF matter to me? You? Depends on your perspective and persuasion. Somewhat embarrassingly, after reading and learning about the IMF for the past few weeks, I still don't have a good understanding of it. The mere fact that it is composed of UN member states, and that the above mentioned Mr. Straus-Kahn is a leader in the French Socialist Party leads me to believe that the interests of free-market economics is not promoted by the IMF. I personally think it is foolish to believe that a handful of politicians of any stripe can control and manage anything as complex as the world economy. At present, the IMF possesses some $375B in assets, of which somewhere around $70B belongs to the taxpayers of The United States, a drop in the bucket, so to speak, considering the vast budget deficits we have to deal with. I don't lose any sleep over the actions of the IMF, but at least feel a bit educated and can talk about it with some confidence at professional gatherings. You?

Lightening Never Strikes Twice...

Not too long ago, a re-airing of "*The World According To Garp*" was on TV. I flipped back and forth among channels and caught portions of the movie. There was one scene where Garp and his wife were wanting to buy a house. As they were looking at a home in particular neighborhood they liked, a small plane overhead was faltering in flight, the engine sputtering and coughing. As they turned to have a look, darned if the four-seater didn't crash right into the second floor of the very home they were looking at, spreading debris all over the place and sending Garp, his wife and the realtor directly onto the deck, audibly praying that no large airplane parts landed on them. As they came to realize that no immediate harm had come to pass, Garp, unbelievably enthusiastic, immediately jumped up on his feet and exclaims, "We'll take it! Honey, it's disaster-proof. Nothing bad can possibly happen again here". And of course, something does...

No one ever knows the future. You hope for good times, but need to plan for, or at least think about, the inevitable bad times. A tragic case in point, one that is certainly an extreme, can only happen in reality, is the sad tale of a Indiana family who, like lightening striking twice in same spot, suffered two individual plane crashes eight years apart, with the same pilot flying either to or from the same vacation home in northern Michigan.

The second crash happened last Friday. Dr. Stephen Hatch, an experienced and avid aviator, was piloting his single engine Beechcraft Bonanza to the family get-a-way on Walloon Lake in northern Michigan. Dr. Hatch, his second wife Kim and one of the family dogs were killed in the crash. Amazingly, Dr. Hatch's son, 16 year old Austin, and his dog Brady, a ashen-colored Labradoodle, survived the impact. Even more amazing, Austin survived almost the exact same crash eight years earlier, on a return flight home from the same family vacation home. In that crash, his mom, 11 year old sister Lindsay and 5 year old brother Ian were killed. His dad escaped with treatable burns, having thrown young Austin from the burning plane as it skidded to a halt after clipping a utility pole just short of Fort Wayne International Airport in September 2003.

Like so much of reality, you just can't make this stuff up. In the profound words of Tom Clancy, *"The difference between fiction and real life is that in fiction the story ultimately has to make sense"*.

Part of my job is to try and imagine the unimaginable. I call it thinking about low-probability but high-impact events. I view my job as one of a risk manager of individual lives, I try to understand and measure different risks that may harm my clients. Some things can never be foreseen, but many can with just an outside eye looking in.

3 Reasons Why Target-Date Funds Are NOT Good...

I gave a speech the other day that talked about choice, personal responsibility and America's seeming love affair with some kind of magic bullet. We all want something for nothing, something easier, something that doesn't actually require *us* to change or think beyond the Final Four. The reality is that life and money are increasingly complex, and every desire, hope and dream we have has some financial component. Wouldn't it be nice if there was some financial product that would work perfectly? Something that didn't require change or thought or concern?

To many, the target-date mutual fund, or sometimes called a lifestyle or freedom fund, is the answer. An easy answer (don't confuse easy with simple...). At least, that's what the mutual fund companies are hoping we will believe. But don't...

What is a target-date mutual fund? It is essentially a fund of many other funds. It is actively managed and shifts allocations over time to a less "aggressive" and more "conservative" stance, so that when you reach your expected retirement age your money is fairly "safe". Let's look at three, all with the target date of 2030...one from Fidelity, one from T. Rowe Price, and one from Charles Schwab, to get an idea of how these funds work...

At the risk of boring the heck out of you, here are the individual objectives as stated by each firm:

Fidelity..."Investing in a combination of underlying Fidelity domestic equity, international equity, bond, and short-term funds using a moderate asset allocation strategy designed for investors expecting to retire around the year 2030. Allocating assets among underlying Fidelity funds according to an asset allocation strategy that becomes increasingly conservative until it reaches approximately 15% in domestic equity funds, 5% in international equity funds, 40% in bond funds, and 40% in short-term funds (approximately 10 to 15 years after the year 2030). Ultimately, the fund will merge with Fidelity Freedom Income Fund."

T. Rowe Price..."To invest in a diversified portfolio of underlying T. Rowe Price mutual funds, consisting of about 90% stocks and 10% bonds for several years, then increasing the allocation to bonds over time. The fund's allocation to stocks will remain fixed at 20% approximately 30 years after its target date."

Schwab..."The investment seeks to provide capital appreciation and income consistent with its current asset allocation. The fund invests primarily in a combination of other Schwab Funds and Laudus Funds. It is designed for an investor who anticipates retiring at or about the target date and plans to withdraw the value of the investor's account in the fund gradually after retirement. At the stated target date, the fund's allocation will be approximately 40% equity securities, 53% fixed income securities, and 7% cash and cash equivalents (including money market funds). It may also invest in unaffiliated third party mutual funds."

Feel better? Have a complete understanding of what is going to happen?

Notice that all three only use funds that are proprietary to the respective mutual fund company. Only Schwab states that it *might* use someone else's fund. Surely, among the vast universe of mutual funds available there would be alternatives that would work better, don't you think? And interestingly, all three start out about the same, but as you can read the endings vary significantly...and it's the ending that counts.

Here are 3 reasons why these funds are not a good choice...

1. It takes a lot of work to really understand what is inside the funds and how allocations change over time.
2. They are typically expensive and underperform.
3. They are not flexible or specific to you...no one knows your situation 3, 5 or 20 years from today.

Looking at item number 1, to understand if any of these is a good choice for you, you actually need to understand the funds that make up the fund. That's a lot of work. Fidelity and Schwab are relatively easy in that they have 21 and 20 holdings respectively, but the T. Rowe Price fund for 2030 has over 4600 holdings. *4600!* For most of us, between 6 and 8 passively-managed index-oriented funds will do a better job over time.

Item number 2 reveals that the average expense ratio of these three target funds is around .76%. Why so much? Well, the target-date fund is actively managed, that is an investment manager makes daily decisions on the makeup of the fund. To add a little insult to injury, most of funds inside the target-date fund are also actively managed...this means you have 2 layers of management expense. For comparison, the average index fund has an expense ratio of under .20%. That little bit of difference will add up to a lot of money over time. And, if you do the homework required in number 1 above, you will know that some of the funds that make up the target-date fund are just plain stinkers...you wouldn't buy them on your own, they'd have no place in your 401k. So, between the higher expense ratio and a few poor performers, you are pretty much doomed to underperformance over time.

The most important reason not to do a target-date fund is they are not flexible with *you. Your* situation, objectives, desires, etc. will change over time. And as your situation, objectives, desires, etc. change, your investment strategy will likely have to change as well. Let's face it, no one knows what is going happen to tomorrow much less 10 years from now. If you want to optimize your outcome, you need to be an active and purposeful participant in your money.

So what is a person to do? If you are the kind of person that doesn't have the time, inclination or expertise to manage your own money, and most of us fit into that category, hire a fee-only advisor. They will more than make up for the fees you pay them by keeping you on track and being flexible. And if you are more of a do-it-yourselfer, 6 to 8 low-cost funds that cover domestic large companies, domestic small companies, developed market (like Great Britain, Germany, Japan, Canada) companies, developing market (like Brazil, India, Turkey, Russia, China) companies, mid-term global bonds, high-yield bonds (also known as junk bonds) and global real estate will do a fine job for you over time.

Nix the target-date funds in your 401k.

The Beast Within...

In the late 1940s and early 1950s, American servicemen stationed in Japan found they were missing something. Something familiar, something comfortable, something pleasing. They were missing the shape and feel of their sweethearts back home. Ever the innovators, Japanese prostitutes quickly began to understand the benefits of silicone and paraffin injections.

And thus a new industry was born...

But not quite so fast. Slowly, over time, and in sporadic bursts, whispers began to spread of what seemed to be an increase in connective-tissue disease among the adventurists, the Japanese prostitutes. Diseases such as rheumatoid arthritis, fibromyalgia and lupus. Stories first appearing in Japanese and Australian medical journals suggested the possibility of a link between these diseases and the implants so coveted by the beneficiaries of sexual favors. As time marched on, a steady drumbeat of anecdotal evidence and innuendo spread east across the Pacific to America. A tipping point so to speak occurred in 1990 with a CBS television airing of *Face to Face with Connie Chung* that featured real woman with real health issues. For the first time, Connie Chung did what no one else had been able to do, she made this issue personal and emotional. And every good pundit, every good speaker and writer, knows that in order to engage an audience, to make them lean forward in their seats with rapt attention, to make them temporarily forget the real world, you have to introduce emotion, you have to make it personal and you have to tell a story. And that is exactly what Connie Chung did.

The problem here is that it was all wrong. There was *no* causality and little correlation between silicone breast implants and the very real and debilitating medical problems of the many women who had received those implants.

So why did we spend millions of dollars researching a problem that did not exist? Why did we waste millions of hours of human capital? Why did we essentially bankrupt an industry? And why did we turn so many people's lives upside down? Why?

Because we are human. Because we allowed the emotional beast that lives deep inside our brain to take charge, to take control, to overrule our rational judgment. We are an emotional species. That is the essence of being human, the ability *to feel*. Unfortunately, life around us has evolved to be far more complex than our basic lizard brain, the limbic system, can handle. What was missing throughout the rise and fall of the silicone breast implant debate was process. *Individual process.* A series of written instructions that help guide emotional beings through certain complex and emotional decision making.

Decisions that are emotionally charged, such as those dealing with health care, end-of-life conversations, money and investing, raising children and the like, have a higher probability of an outcome we desire if there is a *process* at the beginning. Something written down when we are cool-headed and relatively objective that can help guide us to a rational decision, rather than an emotional one.

So, don't wait until a loved one is being wheeled in on a gurney to ICU. Don't wait until someone you care for is cooling to room temperature. Don't wait until your finger is hovering over the mouse, slightly quivering as afflicted with Parkinson's disease to decide if that stock really fits with your objectives and makes sense right now. Don't succumb to gut reactions. Don't be seduced by the emotional beast. Figure it out now, while you can. Have those conversations that need to be had right now. Tonight. Write down your wishes, write down your process. Hold the emotional beast at bay, at least for a bit. Acknowledge its existence, and understand that as human beings we are subject to a variety of built-in and hard-wired biases and emotional motivations. Your outcomes will be better. And your life will be better.

July

"Summer is the time when one sheds one's tensions with one's clothes"

Ada Louise Huxtable

Unanimous Declaration of the Thirteen United States of America...Happy Birthday America

When in the Course of human events it becomes necessary for one people to dissolve the political bands which have connected them with another and to assume among the powers of the earth, the separate and equal station to which the Laws of Nature and of Nature's God entitle them, a decent respect to the opinions of mankind requires that they should declare the causes which impel them to the separation.

We hold these truths to be self-evident, that all men are created equal, that they are endowed by their Creator with certain unalienable Rights, that among these are Life, Liberty and the pursuit of Happiness. — That to secure these rights, Governments are instituted among Men, deriving their just powers from the consent of the governed, — That whenever any Form of Government becomes destructive of these ends, it is the Right of the People to alter or to abolish it, and to institute new Government, laying its foundation on such principles and organizing its powers in such form, as to them shall seem most likely to affect their Safety and Happiness. Prudence, indeed, will dictate that Governments long established should not be changed for light and transient causes; and accordingly all experience hath shewn that mankind are more disposed to suffer, while evils are sufferable than to right themselves by abolishing the forms to which they are accustomed. But when a long train of abuses and usurpations, pursuing invariably the same Object evinces a design to reduce them under absolute Despotism, it is their right, it is their duty, to throw off such Government, and to provide new Guards for their future security. — Such has been the patient sufferance of these Colonies; and such is now the necessity which constrains them to alter their former Systems of Government. The history of the present King of Great Britain is a history of repeated injuries and usurpations, all having in direct object the establishment of an absolute Tyranny over these States. To prove this, let Facts be submitted to a candid world.

He has refused his Assent to Laws, the most wholesome and necessary for the public good.

He has forbidden his Governors to pass Laws of immediate and pressing importance, unless suspended in their operation till his Assent should be obtained; and when so suspended, he has utterly neglected to attend to them.

He has refused to pass other Laws for the accommodation of large districts of people, unless those people would relinquish the right of Representation in the Legislature, a right inestimable to them and formidable to tyrants only.

He has called together legislative bodies at places unusual, uncomfortable, and distant from the depository of their Public Records, for the sole purpose of fatiguing them into compliance with his measures.

He has dissolved Representative Houses repeatedly, for opposing with manly firmness his invasions on the rights of the people.

He has refused for a long time, after such dissolutions,

to cause others to be elected, whereby the Legislative Powers, incapable of Annihilation, have returned to the People at large for their exercise; the State remaining in the mean time exposed to all the dangers of invasion from without, and convulsions within.

He has endeavoured to prevent the population of these States; for that purpose obstructing the Laws for Naturalization of Foreigners; refusing to pass others to encourage their migrations hither, and raising the conditions of new Appropriations of Lands.

He has obstructed the Administration of Justice by refusing his Assent to Laws for establishing Judiciary Powers.

He has made Judges dependent on his Will alone for the tenure of their offices, and the amount and payment of their salaries.

He has erected a multitude of New Offices, and sent hither swarms of Officers to harass our people and eat out their substance.

He has kept among us, in times of peace, Standing Armies without the Consent of our legislatures.

He has affected to render the Military independent of and superior to the Civil Power.

He has combined with others to subject us to a jurisdiction foreign to our constitution, and unacknowledged by our laws; giving his Assent to their Acts of pretended Legislation:

For quartering large bodies of armed troops among us:

For protecting them, by a mock Trial from punishment for any Murders which they should commit on the Inhabitants of these States:

For cutting off our Trade with all parts of the world:

For imposing Taxes on us without our Consent:

For depriving us in many cases, of the benefit of Trial by Jury:

For transporting us beyond Seas to be tried for pretended offences:

For abolishing the free System of English Laws in a neighbouring Province, establishing therein an Arbitrary government, and enlarging its Boundaries so as to render it at once an example and fit instrument for introducing the same absolute rule into these Colonies

For taking away our Charters, abolishing our most valuable Laws and altering fundamentally the Forms of our Governments:

For suspending our own Legislatures, and declaring themselves invested with power to legislate for us in all cases whatsoever.

He has abdicated Government here, by declaring us out of his Protection and waging War against us.

He has plundered our seas, ravaged our coasts, burnt our towns, and destroyed the lives of our people.

He is at this time transporting large Armies of foreign Mercenaries to compleat the works of death, desolation, and tyranny, already begun with circumstances of Cruelty & Perfidy scarcely paralleled in the most barbarous ages, and totally unworthy the Head of a civilized nation.

He has constrained our fellow Citizens taken Captive on the high Seas to bear Arms against their Country, to become the executioners of their friends and Brethren, or to fall themselves by their Hands.

He has excited domestic insurrections amongst us, and has endeavoured to bring on the inhabitants of our frontiers, the merciless Indian Savages whose known rule of warfare, is an undistinguished destruction of all ages, sexes and conditions.

In every stage of these Oppressions We have Petitioned for Redress in the most humble terms: Our repeated Petitions have been answered only by repeated injury. A Prince, whose character is thus marked by every act which may define a Tyrant, is unfit to be the ruler of a free people.

Nor have We been wanting in attentions to our British brethren. We have warned them from time to time of attempts by their legislature to extend an unwarrantable jurisdiction over us. We have reminded them of the circumstances of our emigration and settlement here. We have appealed to their native justice and magnanimity, and we have conjured them by the ties of our common kindred to disavow these usurpations, which would inevitably interrupt our connections and correspondence. They too have been deaf to the voice of justice and of consanguinity. We must, therefore, acquiesce in the necessity, which denounces our Separation, and hold them, as we hold the rest of mankind, Enemies in War, in Peace Friends.

We, therefore, the Representatives of the united States of America, in General Congress, Assembled, appealing to the Supreme Judge of the world for the rectitude of our intentions, do, in the Name, and by Authority of the good People of these Colonies, solemnly publish and declare, That these united Colonies are, and of Right ought to be Free and Independent States, that they are Absolved from all Allegiance to the British Crown, and that all political connection between them and the State of Great Britain, is and ought to be totally dissolved; and that as Free and Independent States, they have full Power to levy War, conclude Peace, contract Alliances, establish Commerce, and to do all other Acts and Things which Independent States may of right do. — And for the support of this Declaration, with a firm reliance on the protection of Divine Providence, we mutually pledge to each other our Lives, our Fortunes, and our sacred Honor.

Baseball Affinity

A recent Forbes magazine had a story about affinity marketing, slick and colorful brochures, and a product too good to be true and too complicated to be understood.

Let's start off with Tom Candiotti. After a 17-year career as a pitcher for major league baseball, he found himself on the short end of investable assets, that is cash and fairly liquid securities, and two young-ish kids to deal with and get though college. Enter retired fellow big-leaguer Todd Stottlemyre, who just happened to have passed his state insurance exam and was now an employee of venerable Merrill Lynch. Stottlemyre convinced Candiotti that Merrill had the perfect product to solve his concerns...

What Stottlemyer and a Merrill insurance and wealth planning specialist pitched was an $18M Variable Life Insurance policy. Actually, the pitch was two policies: one with a $17M face value and the second with a $1.35M face value. Now, a variable life insurance policy is a form of permanent insurance. Inside this type of insurance are a few moving pieces: First, there is the death benefit portion, or face value, that is paid out upon eventual death. Next, there is an investment component with an expected accumulation of cash value, which can be borrowed from the policy. Then, there is the "variable" part, which means that the returns on the investment portion can vary...hopefully, these returns will somewhat mirror the brochure illustrations, but there is no guarantee of that.

At the time, Candiotti was making around $170,000 a year as a broadcaster for the Arizona diamondbacks. No way could he afford the premiums on $18M+ of life insurance. To make all this happen, Merrill enlisted the help of a company called AI Credit. AI would finance the premium payments, allowing Candiotti to get the policies for no money down. According to the policy illustrations (which are just that...illustrations and not fact), the investments inside the life insurance policies would generate enough income to pay off AI's loans. Of course, the loan repayments would deplete any cash value in the policies, but Candiotti would be left with some $18M of death benefits, in force for the rest of his life.

As any of you can guess, this tale doesn't end well for anyone. Stottlemyer states: "My job was to put the firm's (Merrill) specialist in front of the client." Candiotti says, "I didn't ask a lot of questions because I just trusted him (Stottlemyer)." Merrill pushes the can along with: "...(We) encourage clients to seek input and involvement from outside, independent advisors in those strategies."

Not all insurance is bad; there is a place for variable life insurance for some. And not all insurance salespeople are unsavory. But virtually all insurance salespeople earn their income from the commission on the products they sell. And any salesperson will look for an edge to exploit, to leverage their prospecting. That's why they love affinity marketing. Finding some common bond or connection that to one degree or another ties completely independent individuals together is a great introduction. Don't think you have to be someone famous or wealthy to fall for an affinity scheme. Some of the more common affinity ploys come in the form of church or pastor introductions, and involve relatively small amounts of money. Just stay aware and be wary. Remember it's your money on the line.

Fundamental Is as Fundamental Does

Let's take a little trip back in time. I want to re-visit high school science. Remember the periodic chart of elements? It is a tabular display of all the known chemical elements, and is presented by the increasing values of atomic numbers, more specifically by the numbers of protons within a respective nucleus. So, the chart begins in the upper left hand corner with Hydrogen, which has 1 proton. In the bottom right corner is the heaviest known element, Ununoctium, with 118 protons. Let's now flip the chart over so that Ununoctium is on the top left and Hydrogen is on the bottom right. In our new version, the heaviest element is first and the lightest element is last. This is how most investment indexes are assembled, with the largest companies at the top and the smallest companies at the bottom. This is referred to as market-capitalization weighting and means that the largest companies have a greater percentage weight, or representation, in the index than smaller companies. Unlike the natural order of atomic weighting in science, market-cap weighting for investment purposes is purely a human construction. But is it the best way for you to invest your hard earned dollars? Maybe, or maybe not...

Most people think that when they buy a fund that tracks the S&P 500 they are well-diversified and equally invested among America's 500 largest companies. But that is not quite the case. The top 50 companies, or *10% of the index*, represents *over 50% of the index concentration*, and the *top 100 companies represent over 67%.* The bottom 100 companies represent less than 5%, and would have to *move more than 20 times* the movement of the top 100 to have the same impact on the index. So, as it turns out, the S&P 500 is more of a *huge* company index comprised of around *100* huge companies. And that's okay if that is what you want. In truth, market capitalization weighting has an inherent bias that tends to give too much weight to the largest and at times overpriced securities and too little weight to smaller and at times underpriced securities. And this tends to perpetuate the unprofitable behavior of most investors to buy high and sell low.

What are the alternatives?

One alternative is an equal-weight index, where all components have the same representation within the fund. Such a fund was introduced in 2003. The Rydex S&P 500 Equal Weight EFT, **RSP**, has well-outperformed the market-weighted S&P 500, gaining around 80% vs. 40% , over the past 8 years. Of course, 8 years is a relatively short amount of time to judge the soundness of a particular strategy and past performance is not indicative of future results, but so far so good.

I think it gets even a little better. Introduced in 2005 is the fundamental index. Fundamental indexing was developed, tested and put into practice by Rob Arnott and his firm Research Associates. Fundamental indexing weights the individual companies of an index not by size and not equally but by various company fundamentals such as cash flow, book value, dividends and sales. It is in essence a value-weighted index. During test runs, it beat the S&P 500 by some 2% a year over a 43-year time span, and advanced at an annual rate of return of some 5.3% from inception at the end of 2005 through May of this year vs. 3.2% for Vanguard's S&P 500 Index fund. Now that is potentially huge over the long term, and several players such as Power Shares, Schwab and Fidelity have introduced funds that track or mimic Arnott's RAFI indexes. And why not...smaller company and value oriented portfolios have outperformed larger company and growth oriented portfolios over longer periods of time. Not year in and year out, mind you, but over time.

What does this mean for you? Perhaps nothing. Maybe something. Hopefully, you have learned a bit and will want to learn more about what is really in your portfolio and whether what's there is working for your objectives. I like equal weight and fundamental weight indexing. Though they typically carry somewhat higher expense ratios than the traditional market cap weighted index fund, I think they are worth it. If you are interested in learning more, be sure to ask your advisor about the suitability of equal weight and fundamental weight indexing for your particular situation.

The Force Is At Work...

Remember Obi-Wan's explanation after narrowly escaping near certain capture by Imperial Storm Troopers?... *"The Force can have a strong influence on the weak-minded..."*

Not to suggest that too many of us are weak-minded, but *too many of us do stupid things with our money.* Why?

The July 2011 issue of Money magazine had a feature story titled, *"Keeping The Sharks At Bay"*. The feature starts off with the sad tale of 79 year-old Art Tener, a retired service scheduler for a Northern California auto dealer. Lucky Mr. Tener had made a new friend. His new friend escorted him to meals and museums and the like. Turned out that the new friend was an insurance salesman. He suggested that Art take a look at a new deferred annuity. Never mind that this fabulous new product tied up Art's money for up to 16 years, or that Art had a terminal illness that would likely end his life within 2 years, or that Art had to pay $11,000 in penalties out of the $113,000 he rolled from an existing annuity. You see, Art was worried about how he might pay for nursing home care for his wife, who was afflicted with Parkinson's disease. He was led to believe that the new annuity would help. It did not, and because of huge surrender fees built into the new annuity that essentially handcuffed his money, *"instead of enjoying the last nine months of his life, he didn't have $100 to spare."*

I have a relatively new client with a similar but much better ending story. She met an experienced and charismatic insurance salesman who sold her a variable deferred annuity to fund a Roth IRA. Like Mr. Tener, the annuity was wholly unsuitable for her situation, was subject to significant surrender penalties and included high management expense. To add insult to injury, a Roth IRA is *already* a tax advantaged account. Why on earth would anyone put a variable annuity, which provides *tax deferral* on earnings, inside a vehicle that provides *complete tax freedom* on earnings? Luckily, there was not a lot of money involved, so not too much harm or foul, just a little bit *dumb tax*.

Much too often, many of us are unwilling to do the heavy lifting of managing our affairs prudently and asking the difficult questions. Bluntly, we love quick fixes sold with pleasing conversation and million dollar smiles, just sign here for all this to go away. *The Force*, or perhaps more appropriately *The Dark Side* is at times irresistibly seductive. We want to believe.

Believe me, most people *selling* a financial product of any kind need mindful scrutiny. *Always.* And most permanent insurance products and/ or variable or deferred annuities are not suitable for but a select few, typically for folks with high incomes well into six-figures or with a particular situation that can only be solved with insurance.

August

"August was named in honor of Augustus Caesar. It has 31 days because Augustus wanted as many days as Julius Caesar's month of July had"

Unknown

The Big Mo...

Momentum (mō men'tem), *n.*, **1.** force or speed of movement; impetus: *The car* (markets) *gained momentum as it began to go downhill.*

Momentum is a powerful force in the stock market. Once it gains a foothold and traction, it will typically raise a stock or asset class higher than it should go, or drop a stock or asset class lower than it should go. We are now witnessing downward momentum. In a big way. Fear and pessimism has gripped the marke like a cold dread, with hand-wringing anxiety. John Maynard Keynes's haunting refrain lingers in the air: *"Markets can stay irrational longer than you can stay solvent."*

So, what is an investor to do in August 2011?

First, don't panic. Don't succumb to the fear. Don't glue yourself to the TV or your iPhone to catch every nuance of CNBC. Control what you can and do your best to ignore what you can't. This won't last forever.

Second, do evaluate your strategy. Does it still make sense? Do you have sufficient cash and safe savings to ride out a storm? Consider selling some or parts of your weaker or lesser quality holdings. Remember that markets do this; it's part of investing...stocks don't travel in straight lines. But they do trend up over time, so be sure your stock holdings are for longer-term time horizons and don't worry.

Third, salivate a bit. Every serious and experienced investor will have a stash of cash for such an opportunity. The real question now is , *When to buy*? No one can really answer that question, but in a full-fledged panic and strong downward momentum, wait until surprise has passed, wait until anger has passed, wait until despair has passed, wait until investors are wrung out and just don't care anymore. Then look for the tasty and tantalizingly cheap high quality companies you have been wanting to buy, waiting to buy. Or add to your existing high-quality companies.

Fourth, remember every get-out-of-the-market decision is actually two decisions: At some point, you have to decide when to get back in. And for many of us, we get both decisions wrong. I know folks that got out of the market too late, like February or March 2009, and then bought back in, full of optimism, in March or April of 2011.

I don't care how experienced an investor anyone is, it hurts to lose money. Anytime. It's bad enough when we as individuals do something stupid, but it's truly galling when other forces, such as the ineptitude and arrogance of politicians and some bankers, roil what could be and should be a good time. If you find yourself sliding down a hole of darkness, ask yourself: *Would Warren Buffet be selling now? How about Clark Howard?*

This is all easy to say. But, if your strategy is sound and you can *think* through tactical corrections and be flexible without fluster or losing control, then stay with your plan. You *will* get to where you want to go.

The Jubilant/ Despondent Mr. Market

Anyone noticed that the stock market has been a little bipolar lately? It seems that in early August 2011, Mr. Market has not been taking his meds.

The Dow Jones Industrial Average, a price weighted average of 30 US companies, has fallen by some 15% in the last 3 months, more than 10% since the beginning of the month, down around 600 points on Monday, up then down then up over 400 points on Tuesday, down over 500 points yesterday and back up over 400 points today. What is a rational investor to think?

There is only one thing to think, one thing to learn, one fact to take away...*markets are not rational*. Let me repeat, markets are not rational. Markets are driven by people, and people are emotional beings. Beings subject to herd mentality and bouts of irrationality, fear and greed. Perhaps markets are efficient over the long term, that is priced correctly, but certainly not over short time horizons.

Can you find some way to take advantage of human irrationality? To actually make money in a market like this? Two suggestions:

First, if you have a strategy, a process, are paying attention and can keep your mind about you by not following the crowd and succumbing to fear or greed, irrationality can be your friend. Great volatility provides great *opportunity* to buy or sell stocks or funds for a profit. In today's market, you need to be on the lookout for bargains. Look at the fundamentals and valuations. Look for stocks priced cheaper than the intrinsic value of the company. Surely, easier said than done, but there are some genuine opportunities to either purchase good stocks at a good price (and don't confuse a good stock with a good company...not always the same), or add to your existing good stocks or funds. In a falling market such as this, one consumed with fear, buying can take some guts. Remember, any buy or sell must be a part of an overall strategy, a process. It must be a business decision.

Second, for some a Roth conversion might make a lot of sense. To refresh you, a Roth IRA is a tax advantaged account that is funded with after-tax dollars. The great beauty of a Roth is that the *earnings are never taxed*. A conversion occurs when you move money from a traditional IRA to a Roth IRA. This triggers a taxable event, and taxes will need to be paid at your ordinary income tax rate on the amount converted. But, let's say you have an IRA that was worth $50,000 this past May. It is now worth around $40,000. A conversion will only create a taxable event on the $40,000 value, not your previous $50,000 value. And at some point the Roth will gain value back to the $50,000 level, saving you income taxes on $10,000. That gain back to somewhere around fair value is *completely tax free*. And if Mr. Market is stubborn and still forgets to take his meds, you have until October of 2012 to change your mind if you need to, doing what's called a *recharacterization*. A recharacterization is a process where you undo a Roth conversion or contribution and can be performed as late as the IRS will allow to file a tax return, which with extensions is October 15, 2012.

What's the one fact you are supposed to take from this? *Markets are not rational, and opportunities abound in irrationality.*

Systems and Strategies

"Some are born professional traders, some become professional traders, and some have professional trading thrust upon them." So said Edward Oakley Thorpe, PhD. Ed Thorpe is a handsome and smallish man with short, silvery hair. He has an intensely curious nature, and was a bit of a whiz-kid troublemaker growing up. Born in Chicago in 1932, then moving to southern California with his family at the age of 10, he went on to become one of the world's most exceptional, yet virtually unknown to the general public, investors. He is the father of quant finance. That is, using quantitative mathematics and probability theory as a system to place trades in the stock and bond markets.

Ed Thorpe got his start in trading by researching and developing ways to win at gambling, first with roulette, and then moving on to blackjack. When it came to blackjack, he knew instinctively, and eventually proved using probability theory and an IBM 704 computer, that card counting and the law of large numbers would produce profits over time. In actual practice, he was initially bankrolled with $10,000 by a professional gambler and mobster, called Mr. X. Really. Over a warm spring weekend in 1961, he proved his system inside a drab little casino located in Reno, Nevada. He more than doubled his $10,000 stake. His system is really pretty simple, when there are lots of face cards and tens left in the deck, the odds increase that the dealer will bust. You see, in blackjack, the dealer has to take a hit, or draw another card, when their hand totals 16 or less. The more the "10" cards to be dealt, the greater the chances the dealer will draw one and go bust, totaling 22 or more. With a little patience and betting big when the odds swung to his favor, Thorpe was beating the house.

He would soon become *persona non grata* at gambling establishments, often escorted to the parking lot by bulky and grim-faced casino security. Not to fear, though, as Thorpe's fertile mind had already begun working on a new idea, one even more ambitious.

Thorpe parlayed his curious nature and love of probability theory into professional money management. Very successful money management. Thorpe was the first to start a market neutral derivatives hedge fund. He developed a system that was built upon a strategy of exploiting pricing anomalies of various securities. What really set him apart and where so many investors eventually fail is his system took into account the risks inherent in combining money with human behaviors; he was okay sitting on cash when there was nothing tantalizingly apparent, long or short, in the market, and he recognized the forces greed and fear played upon a market. His system had clear and simple buy and sell rules, and was flexible depending upon the above mentioned human behaviors. He claims that from 1970 to mid-1998, his personal investments returned an annual 20% return over the past 28 or so years.

Think about those numbers...20% over 28 years. That is phenomenal. The S&P 500 returned about 8.9% over the same period.

Now, Thorpe has some pretty unique interests and talents; certainly he is an outlier. And the purpose of this piece I've written is not about quant finance so much as the importance of a well-thought out and well-executed system, a strategy that you devise and test and refine over time that makes sense for your abilities and temperament and situation. You obviously can't duplicate Thorpe's system and strategies, but you can learn from him, and take some lessons to apply to your own objectives. If you want to make money in the stock and/ or bond market, or real estate for that matter, you better recognize your own unique interests and talents, and go on to research, develop and implement your own sound strategy. One that recognizes the natural and undeniable risks in dealing with matters involving human emotion; markets are primarily driven by fear and greed, panic and avarice, there is no way to accurately quantify anything as liquid and erratic as the affairs of man. Maintain a disciplined buy and sell methodology. And, be objective, dispassionate, and flexible; become more interested in making money than spending money. The spending fun will come...

A Good Tale...

We all are aware of the "Honey, I shrunk the kids" economy in Michigan. The City of Pontiac, not immune to the realities of post-financial-crash America, was having great difficulty funding the annual $1.5M maintenance tab generated by the shuttered Pontiac Silverdome. Fred Leeb, the city's emergency financial manager, put the facility up for auction in October 2009. Three bids were actually considered, one being an idea to demo the structure and turn the acreage into a landfill. But, the eventual rescuer of the Silverdome from either destruction or fossilization was a Canadian businessman named Andreas Apostolopoulos, a Greek immigrant with a thick accent and little formal education. To me, this is where the story gets interesting....

The aging and idle Silverdome sits among 127 acres of weathered parking lots and narrow strips of weeds on Featherstone Road, along Interstate-75. It's about 30 miles north of Detriot. Originally envisioned by local high school star athlete Don Davidson, the Pontiac Metropolitan Stadium officially opened its doors in 1975. It had seats for 80,311 people, contained 102 luxury suites and cost the citizens of Pontiac $55.7M. It was a covered complex, with a roof of white Teflon-coated fiberglass panels, supported by air pressure from inside the structure. They glinted silver in the sun, hence the nickname "Silverdome". In its glory days, the Silverdome hosted not only the Detroit Lions NFL football team, but also Super Bowl XVI, the Pope, Pink Floyd, Elvis, Bruce Springsteen and the ultimate event of its storied past, André the Giant's visceral challenge of Hulk Hogan in WrestleMania III. Which, by the way, boasted the largest recorded attendance record for a live indoor sporting event in North America. But time and oxidation had taken its toll, and in 2009 Michigan the Silverdome no longer had any meaningful place, purpose or budget.

Let's backtrack a bit to the year 1969. Apostolopoulos, at 17 and traveling alone, left Greece with his suitcase, little cash and limited English. He headed for Toronto, where his married sister lived. He first found work at a Kentucky Fried Chicken, then as a janitor, next started a small business that made plastic garbage bags, and soon after wound his way into the commercial real estate business, buying and leasing income-producing properties. It was in real estate that he really thrived, finding value where no one else did. Ironically, one of his first real estate deals, in 1988, was the purchase of a vacant lot adjacent to a GM auto plant. It seemed reasonable that the plant might need to expand, and indeed within a year, the plant did plan an expansion, and promptly turned his and a partner's $1M investment into $3M. The rest, as they say, is history. His Toronto-based Triple Properties, Inc. is now worth some $800M.

Apostolopoulos was vacationing in his native Greece that fateful October, when his back-at-home son called him on the telephone after noticing an ad in the *Toronto Star* for the soon-to-be held auction of the Silverdome. Intrigued by the possibilities, he flew home directly, and assembled a bid within a couple of days and without *ever* putting foot on the property. His winning bid...$583,000. Again, $583,000. For an 80,000+ seat former NFL football stadium *and* 127 acres of property. Mind boggling. His plans, turn the facility into a professional soccer arena, and make a lot money in the end.

The main point of all this is a story about a man who sees what others do not. Who relies on critical thinking to visualize value. Who is a bit of a contrarian. This is the essence of a value investor. Apostolopoulos built his kingdom brick by brick and step by step with an eye towards and an idea of buying something that either nobody else wants or for less than its intrinsic value. Study Warren Buffet, Marty Whitman, Bruce Berkowitz, Sir John Templeton, Joel Greenblatt or any of a number of successful value investors to learn that objectivity. Avoiding the crowd and a little common sense can reap above market returns for extended periods of time. Really.

Since his purchase, Apostolopoulos invested around $2M to update and renovate the Silverdome, and on April 17, 2010, it re-opened with a monster truck rally. Just last week, on August 6th, the facility hosted professional soccer with a "friendly" rivalry between Italian AC Milano and Greek Panathinaikos FC. Only time will tell us if Andreas Apostolopoulos' keen eye for a deal will pay off. I suspect that it will, the guy knows how to make money. What do you think?

September

*"By all these lovely tokens
September days are here,
With summer's best of weather
And autumn's best of cheer."*

Helen Hunt Jackson

Get To...

The other evening, Thursday in fact, as I was saddling up to go for a ride, my friend and neighbor Bo moseyed over to say hello. We talked about the week, and then the weekend. Bo is a corporate pilot, and gets to fly G4s. He was off this weekend, and we agreed to see each other sometime, most likely Saturday night or Sunday afternoon.

On Friday evening, I attended a concert hosted by another friend and neighbor, Jimmy Casto. Jimmy wrote a song called *"Grateful"*, and performed it that night. As he is singing *"Grateful"*, naturally a song about what he is grateful for, I begin ticking off, one, two, three, four, the things in my life that I'm grateful for. As I am counting off on my fingers, one, two, three, four, my Thursday friend, Bo, is probably grateful for the light Friday evening traffic, as he is being rushed to the emergency room, having suffered a seizure of some sort. It seems he has a tumor growing on the side of his brain, about the same mass as an avocado, with limb-like appendages extending into his sinus cavities. I spoke to him today, Sunday, and had to remind him how he knows me. He told me that he will have exploratory surgery on Tuesday, so the doctors can tell him whether he will make it or not. Just that matter of fact.

As all this is working its way through my mind, I remember an essay I read six or seven months ago entitled *"Get To"*. I can't find it or recall exactly where I came across it, but it goes something like this...

Instead of having to fight the traffic this morning, I *get to*. Instead of having to deal with my teenage son, I *get to.* Instead of having to prospect for new business, I *get to.* Get it?

Trade "have to" for "get to". Make it a habit.

Note: Bo passed away August 22nd, 2012

Greed Is Good

The sequel to Oliver Stone's 1987 masterpiece film *"Wall Street"* opens in theaters today. Tagged *"Wall Street: Money never Sleeps"*, it picks up some 23 years later, just prior to 9/11, as slick manipulator and former master of the universe financier Gordon Gekko, who epitomized the excesses of the 80s, is released from prison. Lucky guy, he's out just in time to participate in new excesses, and experience the tumultuous and exhilarating ride of Wall Street in the new millennium. Gekko, as you may recall, gained notoriety for daring to suggest that *"Greed, for lack of a better word, is good"* as he began a presentation to stakeholders of a company he was taking over.

What is greed? What is fairness? How about justice?

I could bore you with Miriam Webster's definition, but it seems to me these words, or concepts, mean something a little different to each of us. Depending upon our life experiences, political views, employment status and the like, each of us could have vastly different opinions on who and what is greedy, fair or unfair, just or unjust.

Obviously, we all want to live in a world free from greed, where life is fair and justice is always served. Or do we?

I'd like you to consider your own self for a moment. Do you believe that you are successful? Are you self-reliant? Do you have a plan going forward? Are you in control of your life, or is someone or something else responsible for you? The fact is, regardless of what any of us think, and discounting the freak and/ or calamitous physical or mental disaster, each of us is where we are due to the totality of decisions we have made. I repeat, we are where we are because of *our* decisions, and not because of someone else's greed, unfairness or unjustness. This is a reality of life, a part of the human condition, the essence of living on planet Earth. If you accept this universal truth and use it to your advantage, you are more likely to have a view of greed, fairness and justice that does not limit or define who you are. Because the greedy will always be with us, life will never be fair and justice is tenuous at times.

What kind of life would we have if we lived our life to the fullest, utilizing our individual abilities and gifts, taking personal responsibility for our plight, unconcerned with the frivolities of others and without infringing on anyone else's right to life, liberty or property? If we did so, how important, or unimportant, would someone else's greed, fairness or justice be?

Just something to think about...

Want To Be A Landlord? Really?

Many are looking for ways to boost income while staying relatively safe. Some are figuring that rental income from ownership in some present-day inexpensive real estate will fit that bill. After all, home prices are down. And out. I think this is a good time to buy income-producing real estate. If you can.

But how?

Many have tapped out or drawn down cash reserves, and few assets are worth selling at today's depressed prices. So, where to find the cash to take advantage of low, low prices for homes...

How about your IRA?

But not in the sense that many purveyors of self-directed IRAs would have you follow, no, not at all. (A self-directed IRA allows you to invest your retirement money in real estate, gold or silver, a business, most any alternative investment. You have to hire a custodian that specializes in self-directed IRAs. For most of us, they are a poor idea that places retirement money at greater risk of loss and subject to greater expenses).

Why, you ask?

Many reasons. The first of which involves the numerous tax advantages rental real estate affords. Tax advantages like depreciation, like capital gains tax treatment for property held longer than one year, like certain losses offsetting certain gains on other income. All of those tax advantages disappear inside of an IRA.

And any tax deferred money coming out of an IRA *will* be taxed at ordinary income tax rates, regardless of income source.

Next, since the property will be titled in the name of your IRA, not you personally, you can forget about securing any loan for the real estate. No bank will lend to an IRA.

And third, you must maintain funds in the IRA to pay for taxes, maintenance, casualty losses, etc. Often, the *etc.* is what does you in...

Bottom line, if you want to own real estate inside of your IRA, the only thing that makes sense is raw land. There's no depreciation, no casualty losses, no maintenance. Just property taxes.

So, what might make sense for rental property? If you *want* to be a landlord, and I mean really think about what that entails, and the ownership of rental property fits within your portfolio strategy, and you have the income and assets to qualify for a loan, buy the property personally. You can peel off a portion of your IRA into a rollover IRA, one with enough assets to pay the note on your personally held bank note, and set up what is called a *72t election*, which allows you to take a series of equal periodic distributions from your rollover IRA *completely penalty-free.* Tax, of course, will be due, but you can offset the tax due from the IRA distribution with the depreciation, interest, maintenance, etc. for the rental property.

This is not a strategy that fits everyone. But, it might fit you. Want to learn more? Absolutely consult with your tax advisor before jumping in. And be sure you are jumping in the deep end and not the shallow end.

Subject to Misinterpretation...

What's ahead? Deflation, or inflation. Or neither.

Who's read or heard lately about this? There's been a ton of speculation, opinion, blabber, bluster, measured thought and conjecture on what lies ahead for us. Whichever way the cost of living wind blows, our lifestyles and investment portfolios could hang in the balance, like a white-knuckled hang glider with legs swimming through the space above a rocky Pacific shore. The media loves to whip us up into an action hysteria, more ratings for them, more air time for pundits. Interestingly, it seems that the news these days happens so fast, so frenetic, that today's big story or prediction is completely forgotten in two weeks, shredded along with all the other old news. But, when it is so rationally and fervently pronounced, how many of us actually act? Based on what you have heard about future prices, have you bought any gold lately? How about any extra foodstuffs? Ammunition?

So, which way will prices go?

Before I answer that, is anyone mildly interested in how the government defines and calculates cost of living?

Cost of living, simply stated, generally is represented by the Consumer Price Index, or CPI. This index is calculated and reported by the U. S. Bureau of Labor Statistics. There are actually several different CPIs. The most commonly used and referred to is the CPI-U, which reflects the spending patterns of the *average* urban consumer and wage earner, accounting for around 87% of the total U. S. population. To compute the CPI-U, a market basket of goods and services is developed from detailed spending information provided by some 7,000 families across the country. An additional 7,000 or so families keep detailed spending diaries. Also, every month BLS data collectors call or visit thousands of retail outlets, rental units and service providers to obtain pricing information on some 80,000 items within more than 200 categories from 8 major groups. This information is recorded and sent to the national office of BLS where commodity specialists check, verify and adjust the data if necessary. Finally, another sample of around 14,500 families serve as the basis for a Point-of-Purchase survey that identifies where households purchased various types of goods and services. So, the *reported CPI* is the result of a series of interrelated samples that can be *seasonally adjusted to suggest* a measure of *average* cost of living. (I am reminded here of the tale of some poor guy with his head in a baking oven and his feet in ice water. On average, he was fine).

But, there's more. There is the *core* index, which strips out food and energy to "better" represent cost of living. Oddly, housing costs, which make up some 40% of the core index, use assumptions and estimates on the *rental* value of shelter, not actual mortgage costs.

To further muddy the water a bit, there is the Federal Reserve, the body that sets monetary policy designed to combat excessive inflation or deflation. Since February 2000, the Fed's semiannual monetary policy reports to Congress have described the Board's outlook for inflation or deflation in terms of Personal Consumption

Expenditure, or PCE. In explaining its preference for the PCE, the Board stated: *"The chain-type price index for PCE draws extensively on data from the consumer price index but, while not entirely free of measurement problems, has several advantages relative to the CPI. The PCE chain-type index is constructed from a formula that reflects the changing composition of spending and thereby avoids some of the upward bias associated with the fixed-weight nature of the CPI. In addition, the weights are based on a more comprehensive measure of expenditures. Finally, historical data used in the PCE price index can be revised to account for newly available information and for improvements in measurement techniques, including those that affect source data from the CPI; the result is a more consistent series over time."*

Blah, blah, blah...anybody get that?

The end result of all this is a number. A single number. A number that is supposed to tell us which direction we are going and how fast we are traveling. Unfortunately, this number is rearward looking. It is the product of a process. A process that is cumbersome, performed by statisticians and administered by bureaucrats in Washington D. C. It is assembled, analyzed and reported by people. People just like you and me and our neighbors. People with good days and bad days, car wrecks and new cars, pregnant teenagers and graduating seniors. People.

The number is subject to misinterpretation, error and sporadic meddling by self-serving politicians. Though not perfect, it is what it is, and overall does a pretty fair job of estimating and measuring the *average* cost of living in America. But never expect it to be *accurate* for you.

Now, let's get back to the question on everyone's mind, at least on TV, is inflation or deflation ahead?

I'm going to make you wait a little bit longer for that... First, how about next a reasonable definition of each:

Inflation..."*undue expansion or increase of the currency of a country, especially by the issuing of paper money not redeemable in specie; a substantial rise of prices caused by an undue expansion in paper money or bank credit.*"

Deflation..."*an abnormal decline in the level of commodity prices, especially one not accompanied by an equal reduction in the costs of production.*"

Both definitions accurately describe certain events and trends occurring in America today. That's what makes this so darn difficult, the country is awash in near-term uncertainty. Too many as-yet undefined regulations, too many unemployed, too many unknowns. We could tip either way. If you think inflation is going to prevail, load up on all the debt you can, buy hard assets like real estate and gold, buy Treasury Inflation Protected bonds, or TIPs, and keep maturities short on a fixed income securities, or bonds. If you think deflation will prevail, pay off the house and buy a boat load of 30 year bonds. Stocks, by the way, should do okay in either scenario.

The best line I have heard about all this: "*If you happen to know which situation we will get, I could position the portfolio to make a lot of money.*" So said a professional colleague and friend in response to a question from one of his clients.

So, what's ahead? What's the answer?

I don't know. No one does. Believe me. And just because

someone will get it right, don't necessarily assume that person will get it right the next time. What I do know is that everyone is different, with a different set of expectations, objectives and situation. Best to design and implement a strategy that fits *you* going forward, one that is flexible enough to limit losses either way.

October

"October. This is one of the peculiarly dangerous months to speculate in stocks. The others are July, January, September, April, November, May, March, June, December, August, and February."

Mark Twain

What A Day

I love Amazon.

Amazon stock advanced today, October 21, 2010, to $167.97 during trading, the highest price since it went public in 1997. It ended the day at almost $165 per share, up close to 4%. The stock is up over 10,000% since its IPO in 1997. WOW, what a ride.

But, it trades at around 65 times earnings. That is astonishing. Reminiscent of internet mania days. The .com bubble. Most of the stocks I own today trade for around 14 to 17 times earnings, with the highest multiple at 23X.

I can't begin to tell you how many times I have longingly wanted to pull the trigger and buy some Amazon stock. Back in the late 90s, my business partner and I had several discussions about Amazon. Neither one of us really got it, couldn't understand what was driving the stock price toward the stars, it certainly wasn't earnings. We were very tempted to climb on that rocket wagon, but never did.

As with Apple and Microsoft, Amazon's success is due primarily to its highly competitive, sharp-elbowed and notorious micro-manager CEO Jeff Bezos.

Bezos was born in 1964 in Albuquerque, New Mexico. Reportedly, as a toddler he tried to dismantle his crib with a screwdriver, he was quite intense and curious from the start.

His mom was a teenager when she gave birth to him. The marriage with his father lasted little more than one year. When young Jeff was around five, she remarried a Cuban immigrant named Miguel Bezos. The family moved to Miami, and Jeff went to high school there, excelling in science. He went on to study at Princeton University, graduating *summa cum laude*, Phi Beta Kappa with a Bachelor of Science degree in computer technology and electrical engineering. After college, Jeff worked for a couple of Wall Street firms. The story goes that he wrote up the business plan for Amazon while driving cross country to Seattle in 1994. He is obsessive about business process and cost efficiency, loves to read and innovates by focusing on and starting with the customer. For him, this is cultural.

Amazon, the company, reports annual sales that approach $30B. It has virtually no debt and enviable returns on capital. About the only negative is the Lilliputian profit margin of around 3%. Amazon is a marvelous and remarkable enterprise that is likely to be with us for many, many years to come, with plenty of room left to grow.

The last time I seriously thought about buying the stock was back in the spring of 2003. It was selling for around $34 a share. I remember listening to a radio finance show, very respected, hosted by a doctoral professor at Kennesaw State who happened to run his own mutual fund. When a caller asked about Amazon, should he sell or not, the advice was to take his profits and get out. I remembered agreeing with the recommendation. Amazon reported terrific earnings the very next week, and the stock shot up into the $40s. Oh well.

This is the problem with companies we love. We become emotional. I'd have a hard time with Amazon, or even Apple for that matter. I'd worry about whether I should sell and take profits or hang on for a while longer.

I hope I'll own Amazon someday, but probably not. Though I would love to ride that kind of return, talk about a grand slam, I am more comfortable and better at picking solid performers, mostly boring companies that make things people need, and affording me a good night's sleep. I understand what kind of investor I am. I understand my circle of competence and my emotional being. Do you?

Big News...

OMG, it's the first week in October, 2012...Where does the time fly?

Big news! The Dow Jones Industrial Average index rose to its highest point in the past 5 years, trading at around 13,610, up more than 11% since January 3. The Standard & Poor's 500 index rose to close at 1,461, up some 16%, and with 9 out of ten industry groups rising since January 3rd. The Nasdaq composite is doing awesome, up a whopping 20% to 3150+ for the year to date.

So, how did you do? Are you feeling wealthy? Ready to do your part for the economy and spend?

Does it make sense to compare *you* to an index?

Let's review just what an index is...

The Dow Jones Industrial Average is an index (and, BTW, no one can buy an index, only a fund that *tracks* an index, there will always be a difference between the value of an index and the value of a fund. That difference is called a tracking error) of 30 large American based companies. It has been in existence since May of 1896 and is named for Charles Dow and a business associate statistician named Edward Jones (no relationship to Edward Jones Investments). It is a price-weighted index, using a scaled average to compensate for stock splits and other adjustments, the value of the Dow is the sum of the individual company prices divided by a divisor, which changes when there is an adjustment to a component price so as to keep the index value consistent. If you understand that, congratulations. Simply put, the index is based mostly on stock price.

The S&P 500 is a market capitalization-weighted index of the 500 largest companies in America. When most people buy a fund that tracks the S&P 500, they think they are getting a piece of 500 companies. And they are, just not what they typically expect. Because of the market-weighting formula, the larger the company the greater the concentration within the index. The S&P 500 is really more of a S&P 50 because the top 50 companies represent over 50% of the concentration, and the top 100 represent close to 70%. In fact, if you removed Apple, the top dog in the S&P, from the index, the index value would decline by some15%. In other words, Apple alone contributed 15% to the S&P 500's value.

And the NASDAQ, actually the NASDAQ Composite, is also a market capitalization-weighted index of over 3000 companies and other securities traded on NASDAQ exchange. It includes American Depository Receipts (which represent shares of foreign companies in American dollars), Limited Partnerships, Real Estate Investment Trusts and other such instruments. It was launched in 1971. You may recall dot-com-mania, when the index crossed 5000 early in 2000, the index was over-weighted in technology companies because of the market-capitalization weighting.

Notice the emphasis on large? All three of the indexes have this emphasis. And that's perfectly okay if that is what you want. But most people need more. Most people need exposure to small and mid-sized companies, to international companies, to alternative investments.

The point here is don't confuse *you* with the *market*. Remember that the stock market is a market of stocks. What works for one may not work for another. Or for you.

Clash Of The Titans

Northwest Florida, aka the panhandle, is mostly low rolling hills populated with scrub pines, mosquitoes and lots of military personnel. On the east end is Tallahassee, the state capital and home to Florida State University, and the other end is Pensacola, which boasts America's first naval air station and home to the world famous Blue Angels flight demonstration team.

Interstate 10, running east-west, neatly dissects the panhandle area in two, with pristine and welcoming beaches to the south and uninteresting south Georgia and southern Alabama to the north. The climate is humid sub-tropical, with winters not quite warm enough to invite many sun-seeking northerners and summers that beg for gallons of refreshing ice tea.

Northwest Florida is also home to a real estate development company called St. Joe. St. Joe, **JOE**, has been catapulted to headline status as two well-regarded and shrewd investors, David Einhorn of hedge fund Greenlight Capital and Bruce Berkowitz of the value oriented mutual fund Fairholme, battle over the underlying value of the property St. Joe owns there in northwest Florida. Einhorn, naming his company after his wife gave him the "green light" to do so, most recently gained additional fame and fortune, though some would characterize it as notoriety, through a well-publicized short of Lehman Brothers stock prior to its bankruptcy. Berkowitz's Fairholme Fund, **FAIRX**, has *well* outperformed any of the any broad market indexes over the past 10 years

St. Joe owns approximately 580,000 acres in Florida, most of it located in the panhandle area. The stock price enjoyed highs in the lower $80s prior to the financial meltdown and real estate crash, since plummeting to around $16 a share in March 2009. The stock price was rebounding nicely into the middle $30s when the BP Deepwater Horizon exploded, whereupon the price sank, very much like the debris from the oil-drilling platform, into the mid $20s.

Along came Einhorn, who has a well-earned reputation for critical thought and careful analysis, with a compelling 139 page PowerPoint presentation at the Value Investors Congress get-together last week in New York City. He contended that St. Joe has already developed or sold off the most valuable property in its portfolio of acres, and what is left is vastly overvalued on St. Joe's books, somewhat like the bulk of residential mortgages still held by banks. He believes that the company and its holdings should be valued between $7 and $10 a share. As he presented his case, the share price began a new slide, nose-diving below $20 a share over the next two days, losing some 15% of its value.

Well, Bruce Berkowitz, also noted for his well-earned reputation for critical thought and careful analysis, and BTW his Fairholme Fund is the largest shareholder of St. Joe stock, made no formal announcement or statement, but he did double down by buying an additional 3 million shares on the open market at around $22 per share, and reportedly issued a hearty *"thank you"* to Einhorn. St. Joe did issue a statement in rebuttal to Einhorn..."*It is important to understand that an investment in St. Joe is an investment in a company that has a virtually debt-free balance sheet and owns approximately 577,000 acres of land concentrated primarily in Northwest Florida...".*

So where will this drama head, and who will win out in the end? Land, like beauty, is in the eye of the beholder; it is ultimately worth what someone else is willing to pay. I think it is reasonable to believe that both can win, or profit. Berkowitz is patient and has the luxury of time, he's got to be delighted at the opportunity to buy shares that he believes are cheap. Einhorn, on the other hand may have already profited from the stock's 40%+ slide over the past 6 to 8 months. And, he can profit further over the short term with an undeniable action in stock market investing called *momentum*. When a stock price is falling, it tends to keep falling more than it *should*, and vice-versa.

I purchased a bit of St. Joe in August, seemed like a good buy at the time, with the oil leak not damaging the Gulf as much as initially feared. And I sold last week, as I have a portfolio management rule that tries to limits losses. For now, I am content to watch from the sidelines. If I re-purchase St. Joe, it will be on the upswing, where I hopefully will enjoy some *upside* momentum.

72ts and Loans, Oh My!

In the past week or so, four different people have asked me about getting money out of their retirement accounts without any penalty. Generally, this is not advisable for a variety of reasons. But it is possible under certain conditions. If you are intent upon this course of action, there are two ways to do so...a loan from your 401k or other qualified retirement plan and a 72t election from your IRA.

Loans...

1. Must be permitted by the plan. Most qualified retirement plans contain loan provisions...check with your plan administrator.

2. May not exceed $50,000 under any circumstances, or 1/2 of the net present value of your vested account balance, or up to $10,000 even if this is more than 1/2 of your vested account balance.
3. Loans must be repayable within five years, except for loans used to acquire a principal residence for you.
4. The loan must bear a reasonable rate of interest, which in most cases will be considered consumer interest and not deductible unless the loan is secured by a home mortgage.

The two main problems with a loan are:

1. That money is no longer able to grow inside the plan.
2. If you lose your job, the loan must be repaid within 60 days or any outstanding balance will be treated as an early distribution subject to ordinary income taxation and the 10% penalty.

72t Election from an IRA, also known as Substantially Equal Periodic Payments (SEPP)...

1. No age restrictions...available to anyone.
2. The payments, or distributions, must be substantially equal.
3. You must compute the payments as though you intend to distribute the IRA assets over your entire life.
4. You may not discontinue the payments or alter the computation method for at least 5 years *and* reach the age of 59 1/2.

5. The payments, or distributions, are not permitted to be rolled over to another IRA or Roth...they are not "earned income".

The IRS has approved three (3) methods to calculate the annual distribution:

1. Required minimum distribution
2. Fixed amortization
3. Fixed annuitization

With the Required Minimum Distribution method, you determine your retirement account balance and divide it by a life expectancy factor each year. The life expectancy factor can be found in IRS tables; this factor can be based on single life expectancy, Uniform Life Expectancy or joint life expectancy of you and your beneficiary. The amount distributed will vary each year due to changes in the retirement account balance and the life expectancy factor. For example, if your retirement account balance on December 31 of the year before you begin distributions is $350,000 and you are 54 years old and you use the single life expectancy factor of 30.5, your annual distribution will be $11,475.41. let's say that next year, the balance of your retirement account is $360,000, you are 55 years old and the single life expectancy factor is 29.6... your annual distribution will be$12,162.16. Typically, this method will produce a smaller payment initially that will tend to increase over time.

With the Fixed Amortization and Fixed Annuitization method, again you first determine your account balance and which life expectancy table to use. Next, choose an interest rate. IRS safe-harbor guidelines state that you may use any interest rate that does not exceed 120% of the federal midterm rate for either of the two months before the month distributions begin. Right now, interest rates are low, and 120% of the federal midterm rate for 2009 was around 3.2%; the higher the interest rate, the greater the periodic payment. Once you establish your periodic payment, it will not change.

Taking money out of your retirement plan is always a tricky business; there are dozens of gotchas, ifs and ands, and IRS guidelines to be followed to the letter. Be sure you know what you are doing and why, and be sure to look at all of your options first.

November

"November's sky is chill and drear,

November's leaf is red and sear"

Sir Walter Scott

Romney Wins!

What if that was the headline last Wednesday morning, November 7, splashed across front pages of newspapers and web sites across the world? Would *your* world be much different today, this Monday afternoon?

A couple of months ago I hired a telemarketer to help me prospect for my business. I know, I know...a telemarketer. The number 1 objection or stall we heard was, "*I'm waiting until after the election.*" We heard it over and over, and even got people to admit that Washington shouldn't, and *really doesn't*, exert so much influence in their life, that they *themselves* really had the power. Still, they wouldn't budge.

Well, the election is over. Some $2B, that's *billion* as in a *million million*, was spent on this election cycle, and not much has changed. Obama is still the president. The republicans still control the House. And the Democrats still control the Senate. What about you? Who controls you?

The simple fact of the matter is that *you* are the single most important factor in your life, your success, your achievement, your accomplishments. You. Better get used to it.

So, become prepared with a plan for...

1. The Fiscal Cliff: Anybody not know about this? Politicians in Washington, being the dynamic and purposeful leaders they are, have arranged through their constant ineptitude for a series of substantial tax hikes and federal spending cuts to

occur on January 1, 2013. It's like some silly game of chicken. But, there will be some kind of deal, some fix, one or the other will flinch and give way. Trust me. It will not be as bad as it seems, though there will be some change to deal with.

2. Obama Care: Like it or not, *The Patient Protection and Affordable Care Act of 2010* is here. And let's make no mistake, there really is little protection or affordability here, expect for politicians. Take some time to understand how it may affect you, your family and your business or employer.

3. Uncertainty: This is the root of "let's wait" , and causes the most fear. Life is never certain. No one knows what is going to happen in the future. That's what makes life *life*. Uncertainty enhances the human condition. Making the most of what you have today and having a intentional and flexible plan for tomorrow is the absolute best slayer of the fear surrounding uncertainty.

The best way to prepare?

1. Understand your objectives. Sounds simple enough, but for many our objectives really are not that clear, not well-defined, and will change depending upon how we feel at any given moment. Write down your objectives, number 1, 2 and 3. Most important to least important. Not necessarily just financial or money oriented. Objectives that reflect your values and thoughts rather than feelings. Write them down.

2. Become a goal setter and achiever. Goals are the tools that help you achieve your objectives. Like

objectives, goals must be written and specific. Not so much like your objectives, goals must have a time frame, an accountability factor and a deserved reward.

3. Find or develop a sense of humor. Remember the line, "God is a comedian playing to an audience too afraid to laugh"? Learn to laugh and have fun. Practice dancing in the rain.

4. And invest in yourself. Read. Take a class. Write a book. Go meet some people. Do something you always wanted but never have. Make it a practice to invest in yourself on a regular basis. Be challenged.

There will always some obstacle in your way. Someone or something will have a different agenda and/ or objective from you. You job is to find a way around, under, over or through it.

What Would Lincoln Do?

On occasion, I receive inquiries from the media for my opinion on financial topics. I got one a few days ago from blog and media contributor Aaron Crowe, telling me that he was writing a story about Abraham Lincoln and his investments. Completely understandable now that Lincoln is back again in the public eye these days with the new Steven Spielberg movie out, though I find it a bit ironic that Spielberg had to go with a British actor to portray Lincoln...

In any event, Lincoln has been written about more that

any American president, with some 16,000 books and more than a few movies on his life. Not related to this posting, just a fun quote on FB today, "*Lincoln is doing well in theaters. Historically, this has not been true.*"

Back to the point...

Lincoln invested heavily in United States Treasuries. Aaron asked me what I thought of them, and I thought I would share with you my opinion and a few facts about Treasuries:

Treasuries are debt instruments of the United States government. They come in four essential flavors:

1. Treasury bills, or T-bills, mature in less than one year and are sold at a discount to par, or face value. The difference between the discounted purchase price and the face value, or maturity value, equals the interest you will earn if you hold the bill to its maturity, or due date.
2. Treasury Notes, or T-notes, mature in two to ten years. They pay interest twice a year, called coupon payments. You purchase T-notes at face value, and receive your purchase price back at maturity.
3. Treasury Bonds, or long bonds, have maturities from twenty to thirty years. Like a T-note, they pay interest twice a year.
4. TIPS, or Treasury Inflation Protected Securities, are inflation-indexed bonds issued in five year, ten year and thirty year maturities. The face amount, or principal, is adjusted to the Consumer Price Index, or CPI. When the CPI

rises, the principal of the security rises and vice-versa.

The best place to buy treasuries is your bank or TreasuryDirect.com, an online service operated by the Treasury Department.

Now, a little about bonds in general...

Bonds are made up of two components...the price you pay and the interest you receive. As interest rates rise or fall, the value, or price, of bonds goes down or up...it's been really easy to make money on bonds over the past thirty years. In the early 1980s, interest rates were well into double figures, with the prime rate at somewhere around 17%. Imagine a falling interest rate environment, like we've had for the last thirty years. What is a bond worth today, in a 1% return environment that you bought for $1000 and pays you 17%. A lot more than $1000. On the flip side, imagine you buy a bond today for $1000 that pays a 1% coupon, and interest rates rise next year to 3%. You'd have trouble giving that bond away. This is the reality of bond trading. Buying a bond and holding it to its maturity pretty much guarantees what you will make. In reality, you may not want to keep the bond until it matures, and bonds typically will not keep pace with inflation, particularly in a rising interest rate environment. Where do you think interest rates will move over the next 5 or 10 years?

And now, a little about treasuries in specific...

1. The single biggest purchaser of treasuries today is the Federal Reserve, buying some 60% to

80%. Let me repeat that, up to 80% of United States debt obligations are purchased by the Federal Reserve.

2. The next two owners of United States Treasuries are China, with some $1.15T in holdings, and Japan with some $1.12T worth of United States debt.

3. The 10-year treasury yields around 1.55%, which means if you bought the bond today for $1000 and kept it for the full ten years, you will receive your original $1000 back plus 1.55% annual interest payments.

Consider Johnson & Johnson, Exxon-Mobile, Microsoft, even Apple. Today, all of these very well managed and globally operated companies pay a dividend in excess of the coupon payment of a 10 year treasury. If you have a 10 year time horizon, which would you prefer to own?

To be clear, Treasuries are very safe investments. They should make some part of most anyone's investment portfolio. How much depends on that individual's or family's specific situation. Just be sure you understand the risks *and* the rewards...

To Roth or Not To Roth...

Sure am glad the rain came back...I missed it, and last week's sunny warm days were just getting tiresome. Temporarily escaping the dreary wet, I huddled in line at the Starbucks for a hot cup of coffee, with a Wall Street Journal under my arm. It seems that almost every day, there is a piece in the Journal on Roth IRAs. So, here is a short primer...

A Roth IRA is a tax-advantaged IRA, established by the Taxpayer Relief Act (yea, I know...) of 1997 and named for its chief legislative sponsor, Senator William Roth (R) of Delaware. The legislation, section 408A of the tax code, states that all traditional IRA rules apply to Roths except as noted. The exceptions are summarized below:

Four great beauties of a Roth are...

1. The earnings grow tax-free forever, or at least as long as Congress will allow.
2. Your contributions are always available.
3. You can make contributions beyond age 70½ so long as you have earned income, and as long as you are living there will be no required minimum distribution.
4. Lifetime earnings up to $10,000 can be withdrawn penalty and tax free for first time home buyers, those that have not owned a home within the past 24 months.

Now, the downside...

1. All your contributions are after-tax, so ROTHs generally work best for folks in low tax brackets, less than 25%, or for those who expect their future income tax liabilities to increase, or for markets like last spring where asset values were abnormally depressed generally leading to abnormally appreciating values.
2. There are income limitations...for married filing jointly, phase-outs begin at $166,000 in 2009

and $169,000 in 2010, and for single taxpayers phase-outs begin at $105,000 in 2009 and 2010.

3. There is also an income limitation of $100,000 AGI for conversion of traditional IRA assets to a Roth.

4. Earnings withdrawn prior to age 59½, or within 5 years are subject to a 10% penalty and ordinary income tax; the 5 year window for contributions begins on January 1st of the year you first made a contribution, and for conversion amounts the 5 year window resets for each conversion.

Next year, 2010, the government is allowing people with adjusted gross incomes in excess of $100,000 to convert traditional IRA assets to ROTH assets. Any monies converted will be subject to ordinary income tax, though amounts converted can be split evenly over tax years 2010 and 2011; watch out for a tax increase, though, in 2011. A conversion generally makes sense only:

1. For individuals or families who expect their tax liabilities to increase while taking distributions from retirement accounts.

2. If the market tanks next year, 2010, back to or below levels experienced this past March, thus allowing one to enjoy an eventual market rebound at some point in the future tax free.

3. As an estate planning tool for families with very high net worth, concerned about Required Minimum Distributions and/ or generally low retirement account values, that want to pass as much of their wealth as possible along to heirs with as little tax liability as possible.

As with so much in life, be careful what you wish for...this conversion can be a real can-of-worms; be sure that it makes sense for both the short-term and the long-term.

Overall, Roths can be a terrific wealth building tool, but are not for everyone. The best advice is to consult with a trusted advisor before proceeding, and be sure you fully understand all the implications and it fits in with your investment strategy.

Who's Driving Who?

A good friend of mine emailed recently. She's been out of work for over a year now. She's highly skilled, very competent and has always acted with integrity. She's hungry for satisfying and compelling work. She was introduced to a financial services firm that is now recruiting her to become a planner for them, and she asked my opinion. The firm in question is large, profitable and fairly respected. But, *it does not engage in planning or advising*. It is an insurance shop first and foremost. I mean nothing disparaging to insurance companies and their agents, they certainly serve a need, but they are not planners, not advisors and often don't work in their client's best interest. And to advertise themselves as such only serves to confuse an already confused public. In my humble (I learn a little more humility each year, but most that know me well would not use "humble" as an adjective to describe me) opinion, anyway.

So, I thought I would review the differences between financial planners, advisors, money managers, insurance agents and stock brokers.

Let's start with the last, stock brokers. Stock brokers sell securities. They make money, in the form of a commission, on each trade, be it a buy, sell or short transaction. Stock brokers have an obligation to provide *suitable* advice to clients. Stock brokers are registered, either with the state or the SEC or both, and have to pass a background check and various SEC or other regulatory written examinations required for registration. Most stock brokers have no professional designations.

Insurance agents sell life insurance, annuities, variable annuities and shares in mutual funds. There are some insurance agents that truly act as an advisor, but most are salespeople primarily. Like stock brokers, insurance agents make money in the form of a commission on products they sell. Insurance agents have to be registered with the state(s) they practice in, and pass a background check and various written examinations, depending upon the products they sell. Many have no professional designation, but some do, the more common include CLU®, Chartered Life Underwriter, and ChFC®, Chartered Financial Consultant. And, like a stock broker, insurance agents work on a suitability standard with clients.

Money managers manage assets for clients. Their fees are typically a percentage of assets under management, generally in 1% to 2.5% per year range, payable quarterly and based upon asset values at the beginning or end of the quarter. On occasion, and depending upon the circumstances, some money managers also collect a percentage of profits they earn, usually 20%. Most managers have no professional designations, but some do, such as CFA®, Charter Financial Analyst, or CIMA®, Certified Investment Management Analyst. Also included in the money management category is RIA, or Registered Investment Advisor. A RIA, under the Investment Advisors Act of 1940, is legally bound to a *fiduciary* standard in client dealings. A fiduciary *must act in the client's best interest*, as opposed to a mere *suitability* standard.

Financial planners and advisors can be, and sometimes are, all of the above. *I* view a financial planner as one who takes a comprehensive look and approach to minimize financial expense and financial risk for the client, develop a strategy going forward that makes sense for the client's objectives and circumstances, and involves related-field professionals to help accomplish, implement and achieve the desired outcomes of that strategy. About 25% of financial planners have earned the CFP®, or Certified Financial Planner, designation.

A word about designations. There are hundreds of them, most of which mean little. Many are awarded after the payment of fees or tuition, and the passing of an online examination. I view only three as being a gold standard, so to speak. The CFP®, CFA® and ChFC®. These three require the completion of an extensive college and/or graduate-level curriculum, sitting for and passing one to three rigorous multi-day examinations, a minimum three years of documented work experience and a pledge to high ethical standards. Less than 2% of all advisors have earned all three.

The most important qualification of any advisor? Your trust.

Find an advisor that you trust. One that understands your needs and objectives and situation. And be sure that you understand how they get paid and what they are going to do for you. Remember that simple and to the point Cold War and teenager dictum..."*TRUST, BUT VERIFY*". And, *never, ever allow any advisor to have custody of your money.*

December

"April came to bloom and never dim
December

Breathed its killing chills upon the
head or heart."

Robert Louis Stevenson

A Touch of Irony...

What a year. 2010. There's certainly enough to write about. From the economy, to the Tea Party, to the Deep Water Horizon, the Chilean miners, The Patient Protection and Affordable Care Act of 2010, and of course The Dodd-Frank Wall Street Reform and Consumer Protection Act of 2010 (don't you just love how politicians name legislation).

We lost Blake Edwards, Tony Curtis, "Dandy" Don Meredith, Leslie Nielsen, Irvin Kershner, Eddie Fisher, Dan "Rosty" Rostenkowski, John Wooden, Jimmy Dean, Art Linkletter and plenty more.

Here's a little-covered story from 2010, one almost nobody is talking about. A seemingly trivial piece of queer irony...

We have to travel back to the year 2001 to get started. The City of New London, Connecticut wanted to condemn some privately owned land for re-development. The City was going to use eminent domain to take property from local residents living in the waterfront Fort Trumbull neighborhood and transfer the property to a private developer, The New London Development Corporation. New London Development was going to re-develop the property for a "higher and better use" that would generate significant property tax revenues and jobs for the metro New London area. Now, Fort Trumbull was not blighted, mind you, not drug-infested, not a drain on city finances. City politicians were just being opportunistic, looking for ways to enhance the value of living in New London for all of its citizens. Right?

The Fort Trumbull residents resisted the City of New London and sued, galvanized by the passionate outrage of long-time resident and homeowner Susette Kilo. Over several years the case wound its way through state courts to the Supreme Court as *Kilo vs. New London*, and in 2005, on a split 5-4 decision, the Supreme Court sided with the City of New London. To add some insult to injury, and further batter the Fort Trumbull residents, the City of New London actually presented them with invoices for back rent for the 5+ years the case was in dispute, claiming that the property rightly belonged to the City since the original condemnation proceedings.

After national coverage and some intervention by the governor of Connecticut, Jodi Rell, the case was eventually resolved when the City agreed to relocate Kilo's home to a new location, and reluctantly agreed to pay the homeowners substantially more in compensation for their property.

Here's where the irony comes in...

Pharmaceutical giant Pfizer was supposed to be the upscale client of the redevelopment, the ultimate recipient of the city's largesse, behind, of course, New London Development. In late 2009, Pfizer and fellow global pharmaceutical behemoth Wyeth completed a corporate merger. Wyeth, having a major presence in the just-down-the road community of Groton, Connecticut spoiled the plans of New London Development. Pfizer concluded that it made better business sense to consolidate research activities at Wyeth's Groton, CT state of the art campus, and in early 2010 abandoned its plans to deploy research and development in New London. Where Susette Kilo's home once stood is now a vacant lot. There has been no new development. The promised 3000+ jobs and $1M+ annual new tax revenues never materialized. The price tag to the state and city to purchase and bulldoze the condemned property exceeded $78M.

So much for good intentions...

The Fiscal Cliff...

What's dumber than a roomful of politicians?

Nothing. Well, almost nothing...

I've been resistant to talking much about the upcoming "Fiscal Cliff". I've been silent for a number of reasons, mainly that politicians are still debating what they want or can do before January 1, 2013. And next , no one really knows what they will decide, and then the ultimate impact on individuals and families.

The term "Fiscal Cliff" was termed by Ben Bernanke, chairman of the Federal Reserve, in a speech earlier this year.

So, who is Ben Bernanke and the Federal Reserve, what is the Fiscal Cliff, and how will it impact you?

For those that are interested, keep reading, and for those who are not, scroll down a paragraph or two...

The Federal Reserve is an autonomous central banking system authorized by Congress through the Federal

Reserve Act of 1913. The act enumerates three objectives:

1. Maximum Employment
2. Stable Prices, or low inflation
3. Moderate Long-term Interest Rates

The Federal Reserve Act was legislated because of a series of financial panics in the late 1800s and early 1900s, with a particularly disruptive panic in 1907. As part of the act, The Federal Reserve Bank was created as a lender of last resort to banks in the event of depositors withdrawing cash faster than any bank could pay out. The bank is comprised of 12 District Reserve Banks, located in Boston, New York, Richmond, Atlanta, St Louis, Kansas City, Chicago, Minneapolis/ St Paul, Dallas and San Francisco.

A central bank was initially envisioned for America by Alexander Hamilton, the first Secretary of Treasury. His vision has become a series of mandates, from supervising and managing bank institutions to maintaining the financial stability of the United States through the monitoring of inflation rates and such, conducting money policy, such as setting interest rates that banks can borrow at, and creating money, as in today, purchasing vast amounts of United States Treasury obligations.

The Federal Reserve itself is governed by a Board of Governors, all presidential appointees and subject to Senate confirmation for 14-year terms. It is both private and public in nature in that all nationally chartered banks hold stock in the Federal Reserve Bank and as such have a voice in who serves on the Board, yet still is subject to Congressional oversight and any profits go directly to the US Treasury. The chairman of the Federal Reserve is Ben Shalom Bernanke, born December 13, 1953. He served as George W. Bush's chairman of economic advisors and was appointed by Bush to the chair of the Federal Reserve in 2006. President Obama re-nominated him for a 14-year term, and was confirmed by the Senate on January 28, 2010.

The Fiscal Cliff is a combination, a one-two-punch so to speak, of legislated federal tax increases and federal spending decreases. The specifics on taxes...

- *Ordinary income tax rates will change:*
  o The 10% bracket is eliminated.
  o The 25% bracket becomes 28%.
  o The 28% bracket becomes 31%.
  o The 33% bracket becomes 36%.
  o The 35% bracket becomes 39.6%.
- *Investment income tax rates, mostly dividends and long-term capital gains will change:*
  o Capital gains rates will increase for lower income people from 0% to 10% and for higher income people from 15% to 20%.
  o Taxes on dividends will increase from the capital gains rates to ordinary income rates.
  o Individuals with adjusted gross incomes over $200,000 and married taxpayers over $250,000 will pay an additional 3.8% tax on "*unearned*" income.
- *Phase outs*– higher income people will see the return of the personal exemption phase-out and limitations to some itemized deductions. These provisions have been eliminated since 2010.

- *Marriage Penalty* – the higher taxes for two workers making similar amounts of money were eliminated in 2003 but return in 2013 It depends on who makes what as to how much a penalty this will end up being.
- *Coverdell Education Savings Accounts* – these may no longer be used for K-12 expenses and the annual contribution limit reduces to $500 as opposed to the current $2,000.
- *American Opportunity Tax Credit* – this reverts to the less favorable HOPE tax credit.
- *FICA* – the 2% savings most W-2 earners enjoy for their portion (sorry, let's face it...the entire FICA and Medicare payroll tax is a tax on the employee. For the employer portion, that is simply another cost of employment.) goes away, and reverts back to 7.65% .
- *Estate and gift taxes* – the current $5,120,000 exemption will decrease to $1,000,000 and the top rate will increase from 35% to 55%.
- *Depreciation* – the $139,000 immediate deduction of capital purchases reverts to $25,000 and "bonus" depreciation is eliminated.
- *Medicare* – There are two separate items... First, the "*doc fix*" to Medicare will expire, and without it doctors will see their reimbursement for treating Medicare patients reduced by about 27%. Second, the Patient Protection and Affordable Care Act of 2010, otherwise known as *Obamacare*, begins to reduce Medicare spending even further. Without changes to these provisions, fewer doctors will participate in Medicare.

There's more...

- *AMT* – The Alternative Minimum Tax, a separate and parallel income tax originally designed for a very few high income earners but was never adjusted for inflation, will add millions of additional taxpayers subjected to it without a fix.
- *State and local sales tax deductions* – without a retroactive change by the end of the year, taxpayers in states without an income tax will no longer be able to deduct state sales tax on their federal returns.
- *Mortgage insurance premiums* – these premiums were made tax deductible in 2007 and the provision has been extended several times since, but it lapsed at the end of 2011.
- *IRA contributions to charity* – since 2006, taxpayers over age 70½ have been able to contribute directly to charity from their IRAs and have it considered as their required minimum distributions. This year, without this provision, taxpayers who do not itemize or any taxpayers with phase outs based on their Adjusted Gross Income will pay more.

Further, yes, there's more...

Sequestration, which means the *seizure of property for creditors or state*, is part of the penalty in the Budget Control Act of 2011. That penalty mandates cuts in federal spending by some $1.2 trillion beginning in 2013, evenly split between defense and discretionary social spending, such as Social Security, Medicare and veterans benefits.

As of now, the Democrats want to raise taxes, mostly on the wealthy, and impose modest spending cuts, or better stated "reductions in the rate of growth", to reduce the federal deficit. Republicans are opposed to any tax rate changes, but are open to modifications in the tax code, such as a reduction in the mortgage interest deduction and charitable giving deduction for wealthier individuals and families, coupled with "hoped for" pro-growth encouragements to reduce the federal deficit.

How will this impact you? I don't know. It will impact us all to one degree or another, but how much depends upon your specific situation and objectives, and mindset. If you are of a mind to *react* to Washington DC politics instead *responding* to and being flexible, purposeful and intentional, it will probably impact you quite a bit.

The bad news, politicians will always be with us. The good news, we, *you*, are smarter and more innovative than politicians.

Numbers and The Buffett Rule

I like numbers. There's a concreteness to them. I enjoy digging down and understanding what's behind them. I find a sense of order from understanding. The most important lesson I ever learned about numbers was from my dad. He told me to be suspicious of people who use numbers to tell a story. He said that in skilled hands, numbers can tell whatever story the author wants.

Do you think there is more to *The Buffett Rule?* You know the one. The one that President Obama has been touting on his jobs-bill crusade. The one where Warren Buffett thinks it is unfair for him to pay a lower tax rate on his income than his secretary.

Well, I'd like to dig a bit, open the hood and have a generous look-see at the numbers behind Mr. Buffett's claim and President Obama's rhetoric...

First, a couple of definitions:

1. *Earned income* is income a person earns from labor, work, enterprise. Typically, it is reported on a W-2 statement or a 1099. Earned income is taxed at what is referred to as *ordinary income tax rates*, which ranges today from 10% to 35% depending upon how much you earn. It is a progressive tax in that the more you earn, the higher the tax rate on those last dollars of taxable income. (Interest earned is also taxed at ordinary income tax rates)

2. *Investment income* is income earned from investing activities. Typically, it is from investments in capital assets like real estate and stocks. Capital assets held longer than one year are subject to *long-term capital gains tax rates*, which, again depending upon your taxable income, will either be 5% or 15% of the realized gain. (Capital assets held less than one year that sold for a profit are considered short-term capital gains and are taxed as ordinary income)

Warren Buffet makes most of his money from long-term capital investments. His secretary makes most of her money from working for Berkshire Hathaway. So, he is *technically* correct that he pays a lower tax rate than his secretary. But, there are some things he is leaving out, things that opening the hood and looking around with a flashlight will reveal.

Where did Mr. Buffett get the money to invest? Where did it come from? At some point, he had to *earn* it. And pay ordinary income taxes on it.

Let's say that Warren earned $1000. Let's say that his tax rate for those earnings was 25%, and he paid $250 in income tax to the government. That leaves Warren with $750 to invest. Following so far?

Warren then takes his $750 and invests it in ABC, Inc. After one year, his $750 investment is worth $1000. He sells his investment for a $250 profit, or gain. That $250 gain is subject to the long-term capital gains tax rate of 15%. So, Warren owes the government $37.50. Which means that Warren's original $1000 that he earned has now been taxed *twice*, once at the ordinary income tax rate *and* again at the long-term capital gains tax rate. At this point, he has paid some $288 in taxes to the government, or almost *28%*. Not just 15%.

You know that Warren Buffett is going to reinvest his money, right? Then what happens? He holds the investment for at least a year, sells it for a profit, realizes a gain and a new tax. His original $1000 is taxed yet again. And again.

How about another angle of view? Let's say that Warren doesn't sell his investment, but keeps it for a while. He does receive a dividend payment of $100 on his investment in ABC, Inc. (A dividend is an owner's share of profits that the company doesn't need for operations or other investment). That $100 dividend is also subject to a long-term capital gains tax rate of 15%. But, ABC, Inc. had to pay corporate income tax on its earnings before it could ever declare the dividend. Let's say that ABC earned $200. It has a corporate income tax rate of, say 25%, (corporate income tax rates are progressive, just like ordinary income tax rates, and range from 15% to 38%. Unlike what you may believe, most companies pay corporate income tax). Of the $200 earned, ABC gets to keep $150. ABC then pays a dividend to its shareholders of $100, that will be taxed at 15% on the shareholder level as capital gains. But, as you already know, taxes of $50 have already been paid, meaning that of the original $200 earned, the government gets $65, or 32.5%.

One last angle of view. Capital gain income is not indexed for inflation. Let's say that Warren buys a capital asset and holds it for 10 years. He doubles his money over that time, growing $1000 to $2000. Unfortunately, inflation has been growing at around 2% a year. So, he really hasn't doubled his money, his $2000 is only worth $1630. A 7% annualized return has just been knocked down to a real 5%. But, taxes are due on the inflated value. Warren is paying taxes on $370 of phantom value.

There are reasons why investment income is subject to different tax treatment. I'm not saying those reasons are right or wrong, only that they have been left out of the national conversation. And when it comes to numbers, and actually most anything, *never, ever* accept at face value what someone is telling you. Look under the hood. From different perspectives and angles of view. Like my father warned me many, many years ago, in skilled hands numbers can tell any story.

What I Wish For you...

I had a long telephone conversation last night with a dear friend from college. We caught each other up on the past few months of our lives, and had plenty to say. Unfortunately, he told me that his sister, not yet 50, is sick again with cancer. She is not expected to survive this bout.

And so I reflected a bit. Though I have had many challenges this year of 2011, I am happy, healthy and living life each day. There are many that care for me, and most of those I care for are doing well.

My business is helping folks plan for the future. I believe a plan is essential for making the most of what we have right now, and feeling comfortable about what may or may not occur in an unknown future. I find more and more, however, that I am focusing on helping my clients get more out of the present. To realize the blessings they have, and to stay flexible with their plan.

My wish for each and everyone one of you is just that: live in the present and enjoy all the little pleasures that come your way, have a flexible plan for the future and keep smiling.

Merry Christmas...

About Mike Sena, CFP®

Armed with a newly minted BBA degree in finance from the University of Georgia, I set out to awe and conquer the Fortune 500. My first two ventures into large corporate America ended with less than expected results. Fortunately, I inherited an ability from my mom and dad to learn from my mistakes, and figured out pretty quick that big business was not for me. I have been on my own ever since, having started and run several closely-held businesses, where I learned hands-on the value of process, common-sense and flexibility.

My name is Mike Sena and I am a registered investment advisor and an independent fee-only Certified Financial Planner™. I don't sell anything but my skills and experience and advice. I think that helps keep me objective with your money and your life.

You might have detected a theme running though my stories. I have a healthy skepticism of what I read, hear and see. I am wary of insurance salespersons, stock brokers and bankers portraying themselves as *financial advisors,* very few are. I don't much care for actively managed mutual funds, most annuity products, structured financial products put together by banks and brokerage houses, and so on. The list is endless.

Complexity is not your friend nor is it needed for most situations. Business ownership has a great primer, teaching that simpler is almost always better, purposeful flexibility is indispensible and taking your eye off the ball, that is forgetting your priorities, can be calamitous. Over the years, I've come to understand the essentials of business and money, and how to apply them to real life and real people. People just like you.

I'm a loving father, avid and active polo player, speaker and author, happy in my life and definitely *not* your ordinary registered investment advisor.

Follow me on Twitter, @white_street.

Like me at Facebook.com/WhiteStreetAdvisors

Email me Mike@WhiteStreetAdvisors.com

Learn more at WhiteStreetAdvisors.com

Mike Sena, CFP®

37419125R00090

Made in the USA
Charleston, SC
10 January 2015